CULTURE SAVVY
FOR WOMEN

A Complete Guide
To Culturally Correct Behavior
Around The World

Author: Victoria Ugarte
PO Box 3417
Tamarama, NSW 2026
Australia

ABN: 61-119-592-559

Website Links:
www.ExploreMyWorldTravel.com
www.twitter.com/pcardsfrmmillie
www.facebook.com/VictoriaUgarte
Email: victoria@ExploreMyWorldTravel.com

Photo Front Cover: ©iStockphoto.com/15723421
Photo Back Cover: Erica Murray
Editor: Dr. Eduardo F. Ugarte

ISBN: 978-0-9872288-1-9

This book is dedicated to my late mother, Julia Ghezzi Ugarte

6 February, 1922 - 13 January, 2012

For your courage, devotion to family, and the gift of life, thank you.

CULTURE SAVVY
FOR WOMEN

**A Complete Guide
To Culturally Correct Behavior
Around The World**

"Don't leave home without reading this entertaining and informative guide"

"At last we can cross continents confident in the knowledge of how not to offend local sensibilities!

Having travelled extensively I have always wanted to step lightly on foreign soil. It seems utterly logical to me to be respectful of local cultures, however to actually understand the nuances, idiosyncrasies and customs of people is a privilege usually reserved for those living within those societies. Until now.

Culture Savvy For Women is well structured and is truly a fascinating read Each chapter begins with a potted history of the nation – a great introduction or refresher, depending on how much attention you were paying in history class. This enables the traveler to appreciate her surroundings fully before diving in to engage in conversation, gift giving and dining whilst observing the correct etiquette, additionally safe in the knowledge of how to circumvent local taboos. And if one does blunder into unfriendly territory, what safety precautions might come in handy. Don't leave home without reading this entertaining and informative guide, and the world is truly your oyster!"

–Annah Stretton, Fashion Entrepreneur, Director of Stretton Group Ltd, Editor & Publisher of HER, PINK, & WHO'S Who Magazines (NZ)

"Filled to the brim with advice and etiquette tips"

"When you're packing your bags for your next international destination, don't leave this book behind! Filled to the brim with advice and etiquette tips on how to adjust to the cultural norms of your destination, this book will give you the greatest chance of success on your business trips, and ensure many lasting and memorable experiences in your leisure travels. Women around the world will benefit from Victoria's advice."

–**Jen Dalitz, Australia's thought leader on gender balance and author of www.TheSheEOblog.com**

ABOUT THE AUTHOR

Victoria Ugarte, the Intrepid Traveler, is becoming known around the world as one of the most recognized faces of travel and culturally correct behavior.

Her journey to this acclaim started in her country of birth, and childhood, in the Philippines. Raised in Manila in the 1960's, Victoria's father, publisher of defunct national newspaper The Philippines Herald, regularly interacted with foreign dignitaries, businessmen, and expatriates from all over the world, giving Victoria the opportunity to form solid friendships with people from different nationalities.

Being blessed with such a diverse and colorful group of friends, Victoria was exposed to different languages, customs, and cuisines from an early age, giving her the feeling of belonging to the world. At the age of eight, she was bitten by the travel bug when she traveled to Madrid with her family, where she connected with her Spanish roots, and lived for several months.

After migrating to Australia with her family in the 70's, fashion and travel became synonymous with Victoria's career. With over 25 years in the Australian fashion industry, Victoria traveled regularly all over Australia and the world on business, dipping into wonderful and exotic places, as well as more traditional destinations, interacting with people from a wide variety of cultures.

After the Global Financial Crisis of 2007, Victoria felt it was time to hang up her fashion hat and focus on her dual passions, that of traveling and writing.

Ever inspired by the spirit of adventure of her muse, Amelia "Millie" Earhart, Victoria established her widely popular travel blog, Postcards From Millie. Ever the intrepid traveler, she continues to spend 3 months out of every year traveling the world, keeping her readers posted on exciting destinations, latest travel tips, and inspiring them to 'Explore. Discover. Live'.

Victoria has authored three books with Amazon, including *The Travel Bible For Women, and Culture Savvy For Women: A Complete Guide To Culturally Correct Behavior Around The World.*

She regularly publishes travel articles for 'Her Magazine' (NZ) and 'Pink' (NZ). Contact Victoria, wherever she is in the world, to speak at your event or comment in the media by going to www.ExploreMyWorldTravel.com.

TABLE OF CONTENTS

INTRODUCTION

We all have our own stories to tell about the ugly tourist on our travels, don't we. Yes, it's easy to point the finger at "their" bad behavior. And how often have we been repelled by "them," when they have come to visit our own country. Strange and foreign, they flout our conventions, have funny eating habits, and can be downright insulting and rude. Right?

Yet every day, we as tourists pay little heed to foreign customs and unknowingly insult the locals in our travels. We pose for photographs in front of Buddhas and walk into temples with bare arms and legs. We expect native people to perform on demand so that we may record it for posterity. And like animals in a circus, locals continue to perform so that they may be the recipients of the almighty tourist dollar. As tourists, we have the potential to destroy what it is we value in the first place, the world's diversity.

While I've seen more cultural disrespect and intolerance than I care to remember during my travels, I too have been guilty of ignorance about other cultures. Let me share with you such a story…

During the first half of my thirties in the 1990s, I worked as Senior Coordinator for the Leisure Department at the Fashion Office in Myer, Australia's largest department store chain. During my first year on the job, the Fashion Office had me traipsing off to, among other fashion capitals, Tokyo, in search of new trends in style and retail marketing.

The city of Tokyo fascinated me. Raising itself from the ashes of war, Tokyo was, indeed, the City of the Future, blending the very latest in technology with an ancient tradition. Hearing how overwhelming Tokyo can be for a first-time visitor, I was grateful when my company arranged to have a representative from its buying agency accompany me for two days. Despite its modern façade, I was about to find out just how steeped in tradition Japan, and the Japanese, still were.

The job of showing me around Tokyo on my first day fell on Mr Sato (not his real name). In his early forties, Mr Sato was impeccably dressed, formal in manner, and a model of hospitality and professionalism. He accompanied me around Tokyo's fashion districts - Shibuya, Ginza, Harajuku - as I examined department stores and speciality shops.

By 6pm, we were exhausted and agreed that it would be best to continue my retail research the following day. After making our way to the closest train station and hopping on a train to Shinjuku, where my hotel was located, Mr Sato and I fell into conversation. We chatted about Japanese customs, life in Tokyo, and his work at the agency. I then wandered into personal territory by asking Mr Sato if he had a family. *Two children,* was the response, *a boy and a girl.* He asked the same of me, to which I responded, *one boy.* On hearing that I had a son, he gave me a smile and a nod, indicating his approval.

At that stage, I should have considered the culture of the person that I was speaking with and stopped the conversation right there. But because I assumed Mr Sato's values were the same as mine, I volunteered some personal information that would radically change the dynamics of the day.. I shared with him that I was a single mother. On hearing those words, a shadow fell over Mr Sato's face with all the sharpness and speed of a guillotine. I realized at that moment that I had crossed an invisible cultural line - one that I could not step back from.

After expressing his unmistakable disapproval at my "choice of lifestyle", the rest of the train trip was spent in hostile silence. Fifteen minutes later, the doors had barely opened at Shinjuku station when Mr Sato shot off like a rocket, leaving me to fend for myself. Managing to find a taxi rank outside the station, I jumped into the first available taxi, showed the driver a card with the hotel address on it, and sat back in bewilderment. Needless to say, Mr. Sato was not available to accompany me on my retail research the following day. The agency allocated me the services of a lovely young lady, a junior in the organization.

On reflection, I realized that I had mistakenly equated the high-tech surroundings of Tokyo with a Western value system. I was wrong. The cultural chasm between Mr Sato and I was indeed a wide one. In Mr Sato's eyes, my status had plummeted from respected international buyer to disgraced single mother in the span of time that it took me to volunteer the information. In his traditional and patriarchal culture, being in my company caused him to "lose face," the worst thing that can happen to anyone in Japanese society.

So how did I feel? Like Mr Sato, my emotive response to his behavior had been humiliation, indignation, and then judgment. Isn't that what we all tend to do when we come across a cultural perception or practice that we don't understand? And don't we always feel that our opinion is justified? Unless we shift the belief that our country and way of life is the only one worth respecting and adhering to, and that other customs and ways of life are "alien," ignorance will reign and intolerance will prosper.

Knowing what I know today about cultural differences, the first thing that I do whenever I visit any foreign country is research the local culture, its appropriate mores of behavior, and conversation taboos. I then plan to adapt my behavior accordingly. If you don't have the time to do so, then this book will do it for you. The aim of this book then is to paint an overall picture of a particular culture based on its historic influences, and to enlighten you, dear reader, on the mores of its local customs and social etiquette.

Although I don't claim to present a thorough historic account and cultural background on the countries in discussion, I'd like to think that I am able to provide a broad brushstroke of influences based on a nation's historic timeline and heritage. I feel that this is particularly important in trying to understand a culture's social mores.

Before I leave you to enjoy the rest of this book, I'd like to briefly touch upon the safety precautions that I have included in the last section of each country. The information is not meant to represent what is wrong with the culture, or to infer that one culture is less than another. Rather, it is a general reflection of the human condition. Crime and devious behavior is present everywhere, but is much more prevalent in regions that are underprivileged, where offenders are born into environments of extreme poverty and/or discriminated-against minority groups. Thus, it would be irresponsible of me to list the culturally correct behavior for each region without also making the traveler aware of the various dangers and threats that lie waiting within certain community groups.

Having said that, I have always held the belief that respecting local customs and adhering to culturally correct behavior when visiting other lands can bring us closer to bridging the cultural divide. If not, then increased awareness can at least foster tolerance and improve one's personal security while traveling.

Why women only, you may ask. Where I live in Australia, women make up nearly half the business and pleasure travel demographic. According to Tourism Research Australia's *National Visitor Survey,* in 2010, 48% of Australian travelers were women – this includes those traveling domestically and overseas. This percentage can only increase as more women choose to travel on their own. The other reason why I focus on women in this book is that women are far more affected by cultural differences in most parts of the world than their male counterparts.

Although it's unnecessary for women to approach their travels with a spirit of paranoia, it makes sense to be prepared and informed on the art of responsible travel, and that certainly includes being culturally correct in one's behavior. My hope for this book then is to give every woman as many practical tips as possible on the art of culturally correct behavior for a cross-section of cultures. Being "Culture Savvy" means safer and more responsible travel.

In conclusion, travel is not just a great pleasure but also a privilege. A successful trip depends equally on the preparation we make ahead of the trip as well as the precautions we take while we are on our journey. I thank and invite every one of you to go out into the world and explore its four corners, safely, intelligently, sensitively. In doing so, we celebrate the journey and we end up coming home to ourselves

What It Means To Be Culturally Correct

"Life is always walking up to us and saying, 'Come in, the living's fine,' and what do we do? Back off and take its picture."

– RUSSELL BAKER, AMERICAN PULITZER PRIZE-WINNING WRITER.

To answer the question of what it means to be culturally correct, we first need to define "culture." What is it exactly?

Culture is not the product of lone individuals. It's a way of identifying groups of people who share the same language, customs, attitudes, beliefs, and way of life. It has been a powerful human tool for survival since time immemorial. Not only does belonging to a culture give human beings a sense of security, a culture enables a community to teach their young what they have learned in order to survive in their own environment.

The interesting thing is that most people aren't even aware that they have a culture. That is, until they meet someone from another culture. Then it's easy to point out the differences. While there may be differences in the language, customs, behavior, dress, cuisine, and way of life, there may be more drastic differences in the way that people look.

Having defined culture, what does it mean to be culturally correct in our travels?

Cultural correctness in travel has nothing to do with making all the right sounds or being politically correct. It has everything to do with understanding and conserving the cultural heritage of the host communities that we visit on our journey. It is about seeking meaningful connections with local people and adhering to their customs so as not to cause offense. It is about involving the local people in decisions that affect the way that they live, engendering local pride and confidence. It is also being aware of the social issues of one's host community and minimizing any negative impact. Cultural correctness embraces the world's diversity.

Now that we have discussed what it is to be culturally correct, we need to look at its shadow side, which is judgment. And haven't we all been guilty of judgment? How often have we judged someone from a different culture as being rude when they avoided eye contact with us, or nodded their head to everything that we said when in fact they were in disagreement?

Please indulge me while I share with you another story, again from my fashion industry days in the 1990s. This particular story occurred on a flight to London...

My black nylon hand carry weighed a ton. It contained my mini-office, complete with all my paper work, color charts, and reference material that I needed for my retail reconnaissance in London – these were the days before people took their laptop on their travels. (Thank God for wheels!)

Once in the aircraft, I managed to insert my bag into the overhead cabin with some help from the flight steward. Getting it down, however, was going to be another problem. I made a mental note of the 30-something Middle Eastern gentleman seated behind me, dressed in a white cotton galabiyya and a black and white keffiyeh over his head. He was traveling with his young wife and child. Great, I thought. *This man can give me a hand once we've landed.* I settled comfortably into my seat for the long flight ahead.

Twenty-odd hours later, we landed safely in London. Although the flight was smooth and uneventful, my inability to sleep on flights had left me beside myself with exhaustion. I quickly remembered my hand carry in the overhead cabin, which would feel every bit like a sack of bricks after the long haul flight.

After being given the OK to disembark, I maneuvered my way out of my seat, reached up for the overhead cabin, opened it carefully in case anything had moved, and slid my black hand carry halfway out. Turning to the Middle Eastern gentleman in the seat behind me, I politely asked him if he could assist me with my bag.

No reaction. The gentleman looked straight ahead, seemingly not hearing me. *Strange,* I thought. I repeated my request. This time, he lowered his gaze to the ground, continuing not to acknowledge my presence. *He's actually ignoring me,* I thought. An American businessman, who was seated across the aisle from me, immediately took stock of the situation and came to my aid.

As is the case when two different cultures collide, the experience left me with a negative impression of the man and his culture. However, with the benefit of hindsight, education and more life experience, I now know differently. By averting his eyes and not engaging me in conversation, the said gentleman was showing me respect in the Muslim tradition. In the Middle Eastern Muslim tradition, it is unacceptable for a man to touch or gaze at a woman who is not his wife or a close family member, as both these acts are considered intimate acts.

That experience seemed like a lifetime ago, when I traveled the world frequently but not necessarily sensitively. *Mea Culpa.* Today, with so much information easily available over the internet, there is no excuse. And yet many still travel the world with the notion that a different culture is a lesser one. It is all too easy to lump any culture that we come in contact with into an imaginary category that we have constructed in our own minds, based on judgment and a flawed perception.

Let us never forget, therefore, as we journey through other countries and cultures, that we are dealing with actual people, with individuals. If I were to give any words of advice on becoming culture savvy, it would be this: Understand it, work with it, learn from it.

Want access to a BONUS eBook on 'How To Enrich Your Life Through Travel'?

Go to www.ExploreMyWorldTravel.com/bonus-download now to get your copy of 'How To Enrich Your Life Through Travel', absolutely FREE.

two

Australia

"You feel free in Australia. There is great relief in the atmosphere—a relief from tension, from pressure, an absence of control of will or form. The Skies open above you and the areas open around you."

– D.H LAWRENCE, ENGLISH NOVELIST, POET, PLAYWRIGHT, ESSAYIST, LITERARY CRITIC AND PAINTER

Historic Influences:

Australia is a modern nation state with an ancient heritage. With a long and colorful history that is rich in cultural diversity, its origins have helped to mold the psyche of the present day Australian.

When we speak of ancient civilizations, Egypt, Mesopotamia, and Greece always comes to mind. And yet, the Indigenous peoples of Australia inhabited the continent up to 60,000 years prior to the arrival of the white settlers towards the end of the 1700s. To help you put it in perspective, the Aboriginal culture pre-dated the cave art in Lascaux (France) and the pyramids of Egypt by tens of thousands of years. With its highly developed tradition founded on a deep connection with the land, the Australian Aboriginal can claim to be the oldest continuously living culture on the planet.

Australia entered its phase as a penal colony in 1788, when Britain shipped 850 convicts and their marine guards and officers over in a desperate bid to alleviate their overflowing prisons at a time of social unrest. Sydney's first free settlers arrived five years later in the form of five single men and two families, bringing to the savage terrain a pioneering spirit and an eagerness to embrace change. After the convicts were given pardons on completion of their sentences, they were allocated parcels of land to farm. Thus began Australia's convict heritage.

Rather than a single British colony, Australia originally consisted of six separate colonies. These colonies became the Federation Of Australian States, which eventually came together to form the Commonwealth of Australia in 1901.

Australia's Post Federation Period was marked by great upheaval. With its involvement in 2 world wars, more armed conflict in the Korean and Vietnam Wars, and the Great Depression, it was sport that provided millions of Australians with respite from misery and much needed hope. This was a period marked by sporting greats such as Sir Donald Bradman, one of the greatest cricketers of all time, and Rod Laver, the only person in history to have won the Grand Slam twice (1962 and 1969).

Millions have since migrated to Australia's pristine shores from Asia, Europe, and the Middle East, making Australia the colorful and exciting multi-cultural nation it is today. Australia considers itself a true democracy, where fundamental rights are largely respected and freedom of thought and expression still upheld.

The Australian Concept of Mateship:

The qualities that people the world over can identify with an Australian are their relaxed approach to life, egalitarian values, and concept of mateship. The values of mateship stem from Australia's convict and colonial past, when people struggled against a harsh and unfamiliar land, and often against an unjust authority.

Frequently heard as a greeting - as in "G'day mate" - the word "mate" was originally used by convicts, gold miners, and diggers in the world wars, where a man had to stick by his mates and not let them down if he was to get by. With a far stronger meaning than the word "friend", a "mate" means mutual respect and support, no matter what the circumstances. A colloquialism that is very commonly used by Australian males, it crosses boundaries from CEOs of multi-billion dollar corporations to the derelict on the street. With the younger generation, the word "mate" is no longer even sex specific, with many girls and women using the term freely with their close friends, whether male or female.

The Australian Accent:

About 20% of Australian males speak with a broad accent that is a blend of the English, Irish, and the Scot that has evolved over time. While many foreigners may find it "unsophisticated" and difficult to understand, any Aussie will tell you that their accent is normal and everyone else's accent sounds funny.

Unlike other countries, the Australian accent is not class specific, nor is it a reflection of one's level of education or breeding, if you are a male. The late multi billionaire, Kerry Packer spoke with just as broad an accent as the builder down the road. However, it is interesting to note that it is rare, and more unacceptable, for educated women in Australia to speak with as broad an accent, an exception to Australia's egalitarian and non-sexist ideals.

Greeting & Conversation Etiquette:

"Australians appear very naïve to the newly arrived Japanese. They speak the same with everyone."

– HIRO MUKAI, SPEAKER AT A 1980 PREFECTURE.

The average Australian is laid back, down to earth, and holds very strong egalitarian values, which directly translates in the way that they relate to each other and the rest of the world. They tend to be suspicious of any form of pretentiousness and arrogance, and have little respect for formalities or self-aggrandizement. They tend to judge a person's competence and character through their actions rather than their words.

When it comes to social etiquette, the Australians differ from those of other cultures in that more emphasis is placed on expressing equality than becoming preoccupied with what title to use when addressing someone, or how to hold a knife and fork. It pays to bear this in mind when visiting Australia.

When meeting someone for the first time in a social or business setting, an Australian will normally shake hands while maintaining direct eye contact. The hand shake is moderately firm. While some men may not initiate a hand shake with a woman, it is perfectly acceptable for a woman to initiate the handshake with a man. Once they get to know you better, most Australians will kiss once on the right cheek, particularly among women, and sometimes women with men. Men never kiss each other in Australia.

After the initial greeting, Australians will tend to move quickly to a first-name basis, even in business. A more formal greeting, such as Mr/Mrs/Ms followed by the person's surname, is normally reserved for official occasions. Out of respect and to avoid being viewed as presumptuous, however, it's best to wait for your Australian colleague to initiate the transition to a first-name basis.

Australia's strong egalitarian attitude strongly influences how professional and/or academic titles are viewed in Australian society; while professional qualifications and experience are highly valued, titles do not necessarily command the same respect as they do in other countries. Therefore, pushing the weight of your title around is a definite *faux pas,* and can lead you to being labeled pretentious. And while we're at it, obvious displays of wealth are wasted on the Aussies. In fact, they will view it with disdain or suspicion.

This relaxed approach of the Australian towards titles and dignitaries has been known to cause problems with some international visitors, who often feel that more respect is warranted. Exacerbating the problem, Australians are often oblivious to the fact that they have caused offense in others because they are so difficult to offend themselves. This has led many foreigners to label Australians as ignorant and uneducated. If the truth be known, Australians see themselves on an equal footing with everyone, from the man on the street to the Queen of England. Speaking of the Queen of England, the English were horrified in the 1970s when Australian cricketing great, Dennis Lillee greeted HM Queen Elizabeth II with the line, "G'day, how ya going?" when introduced to her. While the English press was horrified and labeled Lillee an ignorant buffoon, in Lillee's egalitarian eyes he merely saw himself as Her Majesty's equal. While Australians today are far more respectful and sensitive to cultural protocol than Dennis Lillee was in the 1970s, there is still a very strong egalitarian edge to the Australian national identity.

In conversation, Australians prefer direct eye contact as they see it as a sign of respect and an indication that the person is listening. Their communication style is direct, frank and straightforward, with little regard for non-verbal cues. Most Australians do not hesitate to say a straight but polite "no."

The Australians are similar to the English in that they tend to think that people who do not say "please" or "thank you" are rude. "Excuse me" is commonly used to get a person's attention, and "sorry" is employed when they bump into someone. When someone sneezes, people in Australia normally say, "bless you," which does not have any religious connotation.

In conversation, Australians enjoy a healthy debate and are happy to hear other opinions if they are presented respectfully and with good humor. They will talk incessantly about the weather, sports, and local politics. Any topic related to Australia is a good topic of conversation so long as the other person is sincere and informed. It is considered poor form for anyone to lose their cool or become overly aggressive in a discussion.

The Aussie sense of humor can best be described as mischievous and robust. While people from other nationalities usually make a joke about someone when the other person isn't present in the conversation, the opposite is the case in Australia. Australians will have no qualms about good naturedly teasing or ridiculing another person in front of them. In fact you'll know they've developed a liking to you when they do. The joke is never malicious, it's not meant to offend, and you are expected to take the joke in the spirit that it is given and reply in kind. However, while the British are well practiced at volleying good natured "insults" due to their dry wit and love of irony, Americans and Asians tend to have a little more trouble with this custom of teasing, often referred to as "taking the Mickey" or more crudely "taking the piss."

If you find it hard to reply to someone's teasing, just have a chuckle and change the subject. Showing that the joke caused you offense may only encourage your Australian friend to keep going. And may I recommend that you don't start trading insults with Australians until you get to know them a little better first. That way, you will know exactly which topics are off limits and which are fair game.

Conversation Taboos:

"I can personally affirm that to stand before an audience of beaming Australians and make even the mildest quip about a convict past is to feel the air conditioning immediately elevated."

– BILL BRYSON, AMERICAN AUTHOR

Boasting about yourself or your accomplishments, or how much money you make, will be viewed with skepticism, suspicion, and distaste in Australia. Neither should you make exaggerated claims or adopt a verbose tone. The tall poppy syndrome is alive and well in the Australian culture, and Aussies prefer not to draw attention to their qualifications or personal achievements. They prefer to let the achievements speak for themselves.

While Australians like to joke about themselves with each other, they will not find it funny if an outsider decides to laugh at or put down their country or culture. Australians are proud of their country and way of life and will let you know straight away if you have "crossed the line."

Discussing politics and sharing your views is OK, so long as you are informed and are not out to criticize. Avoid getting into a heated debate over politics, however. Losing your cool, or staying on a subject for too long, is not seen as good form.

Similar to the Americans and the British, stay away from discussions on sex and religion in either a social or business setting in

Australia. It is in equally poor taste to remark about Australia's history as a penal colony, make racist comments, or to speak about the Australian Aborigines in a derogatory manner.

Australian Slang:

Australians are fond of using shortened versions of longer words. In fact, they've elevated it into an art form. While I won't go into where each word originated from, I'll tell you what they mean.

If you don't understand the word when you hear it, Australians will only be too happy to explain it, and even laugh about it with you. Here are a few of the more common expressions:

- Arvo – "Arvo" means "afternoon", as in "See you this arvo."

- Barbie – This does not refer to the popular doll by Mattel. As traditional for the Australian as High Tea is for the English, "barbie" means a barbecue and is an extremely casual affair. Occurring at a picnic park, the beach, or in someone's backyard, "barbies" consist of steaks and sausages, served with salads and bread rolls. Guests may often be asked to bring their own meat and alcohol.

- Bloke – "Bloke" refers to a man, as in "Go see that bloke over there for directions."

- Bludge – This word means to be lazy. This can also mean a really easy job, as in "The work was such a bludge, so I finished early." To be called a "bludger" in Australia is an insult, as it means that you're someone who takes without giving anything back.

- Bring a plate – When invited to someone's home for a barbecue, you may be asked to "bring a plate." This most definitely does not mean bringing your own crockery and cutlery. It means to bring a dish to share with the other guests. If you're unsure of what to bring, then ask your host for suggestions.

- BYO – This means "bring your own" and refers to alcohol, usually wine or beer. BYO applies if you are invited to a casual barbecue and the host would like you to bring your alcohol of choice for you to enjoy, and perhaps share with others in the group. If you don't drink alcohol, then you can bring any non-alcoholic beverage that you enjoy. There are also BYO restaurants, where you can bring your own wine, although they usually charge a small corkage fee.

- Chook – This is the shortened version of "chicken," as in "We're having roast chook for dinner."

- Crook – Crook means to be sick or ill, as in "I was crook all weekend."

- Cuppa – This refers to a cup of tea or coffee. "Drop by this arvo for a cuppa" means "Come by this afternoon for a cup of tea or coffee."

- Fair dinkum – "Fair dinkum" is an old Australian saying which means, "It's the truth." You can still hear many Aussies peppering their conversation with "fair dinkum?", meaning, "Is it really true?"

- Flat out – This means "really busy", as in "I was flat out this morning!"

- Fortnight – This means two weeks. Many employees in Australia are paid fortnightly, meaning every two weeks.

- Loo – "Loo" is a colloquial term for toilet. While it is more polite to ask "May I use your toilet, please?" when visiting someone's home for the first time, once people have gotten to know each other better, it's common for people to ask "Where's the loo?"

- Mate – A "mate" to an Australian is not just a friend, but someone who will stick by you through thick and thin. Australian men often address each other as "mate" in less formal situations, whether they know each other or not, although women have started to use it too. The history and sentiment behind this word runs deep in the Australian psyche, so being considered a "mate" in an Australian's mind is a great privilege.

- Ow-ya-goin? – Pronounced as it is written, this means "How are you?", and usually has "mate" thrown in at the end of it. This is a colloquial exchange between friends, usually male. It is never used in a business or formal setting.

- Piss or Grog – The words "piss" or "grog" refer to alcohol. Someone getting "on the piss" or "on the grog" means going on a drinking spree. Unlike the United States, where someone "getting pissed" means that they're getting angry, in Australia, it means that they're getting drunk.

- Thongs – Unlike the American translation, which refers to an extremely brief undergarment, "thongs" in Australia means flip flops or slippers, which is costume de rigueur for the beach.

- Taking the piss - Although not a polite expression, "taking the piss" out of someone means to tease someone good naturedly.

- Shout or round – You'll hear the expression "Let me shout you a drink" when you're at a bar or pub with your Aussie friends. This means they'd like to buy you a drink. It's usual for each person to "shout a round," which means that each person takes a turn at buying every person in the group a drink. If you don't drink, it's perfectly OK to say so at the beginning. You will then not be obliged to "shout a round". The shout does not apply to nightclubs, however, where drinks can be expensive.

- Snag – "Snags" mean sausages, whether they're made of pork, beef or chicken.

- Tea – Like in parts of Britain, "tea" can also mean dinner. So if you happen to be asked by a friend to "Come over for tea at 6pm," you can safely assume it will be for dinner.

- Where to go – Telling someone "where to go" does not mean that you're giving them friendly directions. It's the equivalent of telling someone to "go jump."

- Whingeing – "Whingeing" means to complain incessantly. To be called a "whinger" in Australia is a definite insult. It can many times refer to people from other countries who come to Australia and continually complain about the Aussie way of life.

Appropriate Social Behavior:

A trait that stems from their colonial past, Australians have a love of order, which includes standing in line, or "queues" as it is often called. Australians will wait patiently for their turn in a queue, no matter how long it takes, so don't even think about skipping to the front when boarding a bus, waiting in line for a taxi, or waiting to be served at the post office, bank, or store. And despite their famous laid back attitude and "no worries" culture, Australians are fairly punctual, especially when it comes to social invitations and business. If you know that you are going to be late for a social or business engagement, try to contact your host or colleague to let them know as soon as possible.

Silent composure under suffering has etched itself into the Australian psyche since the days of the convicts, which is the reason why Australians love the underdog and the "battler," someone who stands up for themselves in the face of adversity. They have little regard for a victim mentality or subservient attitude. If you feel the need to talk about your problems, then throw a little humor into the mix. Aussies will appreciate your "no worries" attitude far more than your lamentations.

If you haven't driven in Australia before, remember that Australians drive on the left-hand side of the road, with vehicles overtaking from the right. Overall, Australians are fairly orderly, with a healthy respect for rules and regulations. However, they are also impatient and not as polite as Americans, so you may get the occasional "finger," or hand on the horn, if you happen to forget your indicator when making a turn or stop abruptly. Don't take it personally. Just hold your hand up in apology and continue on your way.

Australians are really passionate about their beaches. In fact, they are akin to sacred ground, and the quickest way to get on the wrong side of any Aussie is to leave your rubbish on the beach. Treat the beach as you would your own home and dispose of your rubbish thoughtfully in the council bins provided as you leave.

Gift Giving Etiquette:

Gift-giving is not part of Australian business culture, so it is best not to send a gift to your business counterpart unless you receive one first. However, a social invitation to someone's home is another story and it is considered bad form to arrive empty handed.

You may bring a token gift of flowers, chocolates, a piece of handicraft from your country, or a good bottle of wine. Avoid giving expensive gifts as it will only make your host uncomfortable. Rather, your thoughtful choice will be considered more important than the cost of the gift itself.

If you are bringing a bottle of wine to a dinner invitation, never discuss the cost of the wine. If the wine is not drunk at the dinner, it is polite to leave it as a gift for the host. It is a faux pas to take it back with you.

Dining Etiquette:

"In my early days in Australia, I was invited to a housewarming at a colleague's place and told to 'bring a plate'. Coming from the Philippines where this is an unusual request, my husband and I thought it was because our colleague did not have the amount of china needed for such an occasion. So I not only brought plates for my husband and I but some cutlery for good measure! I still get ribbed about this more than 30 years later!"

– MARICHIT BERNARDO, MIGRATED TO AUSTRALIA FROM THE PHILIPPINES IN THE 1970S.

Whether a barbecue or a more formal dinner party, there is nothing an Australian loves more than to invite a group of friends over to their home for a meal and a few drinks. Advise your host of your dietary requirements straight away, whether you are vegetarian or don't eat certain foods because of specific allergies or your religion. You'll find that Australians are very accommodating and respectful towards other people's cultures and customs.

Aussies are not as relaxed with time as people from Latin America or the Mediterranean. If a social invitation stipulates a 7:30pm arrival, it's acceptable to arrive at 7:45. Any later than that, however, requires a quick call to your host. If it's an official engagement that you are invited to, then punctuality is a must.

When you are invited to a less formal party, you may be asked to "bring a plate." This means that you have been asked to bring a dish to share with your host and the other guests. Check with your host as to what to bring, as they'll have an idea what the other guests will be bringing. Bringing something traditional from your country of origin is always a great idea, as Australians are more adventurous than most cultures with international cuisines.

The food in an Australian household may be prepared and served one of several ways:

- Passing the serving platters from one guest to another, so that they may serve themselves.

- Buffet style, so that guests may serve themselves - usually reserved for larger numbers.

- The host plates the food individually from the kitchen and passes it to each person.

Guests usually wait until everyone at their table has been served before they begin to eat, with an exception made for very large groups.

Food is eaten Continental style, with a knife and fork, using the cutlery from the outside of the layout first, working your way inward to the utensils closest to the plate. To indicate that you have finished eating, lay your knife and fork parallel on your plate with the handles facing to the right. Keep your elbows off the table and your hands above the table when eating.

If an Aussie group of friends go out to dine at a restaurant, the bill is split evenly among the diners, men and women. Exceptions do apply, of course. For example, when one is invited to dine out (e.g., a date, or a reciprocal invitation), the one inviting usually pays for the meal. In business, the bill may sometimes be picked up as a way to foster a good relationship. However, once a relationship has been established, then it's normal for everyone to pay for their own meal (ie., going "Dutch").

What's So Special About Vegemite?

While the rest of the world scratches its head, trying to figure out how anyone can eat anything so vile, Australians won't hear a word against Vegemite. In fact, they'll tell you that you're probably eating it the wrong way or spreading it on too thick. Chances are, they're right.

Similar to England's Marmite, Vegemite was invented in 1922 by food technologist Dr Cyril Callister following the disruption of British Marmite production after World War I, when he was asked by his employer, Fred Walker & Co, to develop a spread from the used yeast being dumped by breweries. And so Vegemite was born and has been making Aussie cheeks pucker ever since.

Dark brown in color, and never to be mistaken for chocolate, Vegemite is a food paste made from yeast extract that is salty in flavor and used for spreading over sandwiches, biscuits, crackers, and toast. Despite its huge salt content, it has many health benefits. A piece of bread with Vegemite lightly spread over it can give you almost a quarter of your daily niacin requirement, a third of your daily riboflavin intake, biotin and a healthy dose of vitamins B1 and B6.

Here's a tip when eating Vegemite: It is definitely an acquired taste so start small. Ideally, you should spread some butter over the piece of toast or cracker first, then a very thin layer of Vegemite over the butter. Make sure that you can see some butter through the Vegemite. If you cannot, then you may have spread it on too thick. You can always add more Vegemite once you've gotten used to the flavor. Lastly, remember that it isn't peanut butter, so avoid eating it out of the jar with a spoon.

Drinking Etiquette:

Although Australians are, in general, welcoming and easy going, it may take a while for you to be accepted into their inner circle of friends. The custom of "sharing a round" or "a shout" at the pub is a great opportunity for any outsider to be inducted into a closed social clique and treated as an equal.

A "round" or "shout" is where one individual pays for the other drinks of the drinking party. Once the drinks have been consumed, then it's the next person's turn to pay for the next round or shout. Every member of the drinking party must buy the same number of rounds, regardless of gender, financial status, or origin. Failure to uphold one's round is considered poor form, showing a weakness in character, frugality of spirit, and failure to stand up to an unspoken commitment. And chances are you'll never be included again. In Australia, a lone woman can go out drinking with the boys, and provided she buys her round she will be treated as one of the boys.

BYO in Australia means to "bring your own" drink, either alcoholic or non-alcoholic, to a casual get together like a picnic or barbecue. Some restaurants are BYO, meaning that you can bring your own wine when coming to dine. A small corkage fee is charged for providing and cleaning glasses. It is always a good idea to bring your own wine to BYO restaurants, as wines sold in

Australian restaurants can be expensive in comparison to other countries.

Dressing Etiquette:

The days of Australian's being scruffy dressers are over. Australian men and women follow fashion trends just as avidly as any other person in the Western world. However, also remember that Australia has a very strong outdoor lifestyle and beach culture which influences their fashion choices in a major way. These factors make for more relaxed, casual, understated, and unstructured wardrobe choices. And while we're on the topic, Australian's down-to-earth nature and aversion for any overt displays of wealth extends to fashion. Labels and status symbols are OK in Oz, but try not to deck yourself from head to toe in them or you risk looking like a "fashion victim" or "try hard".

During the summer months, most Australians enjoy barbecues and picnics outdoors, and descend to the coastline and beaches for a swim. On hot days, Aussies may wear little clothing. The wearing of little clothing in the summer is in no way a reflection of the lack of moral standards in Australia. Rather, it is a sign of practical dress for a life lived in the outdoors and under a harsh sun.

For dinner invitations at someone's home or dining out, a smart casual style is quite acceptable, meaning an elegant dress or skirt/ tailored pants and top for women. "Smart casual" never means jeans, shorts, thongs (slippers) or tracksuits (sweats). If an invitation is formal, it will always be spelled out. Ask your host what the dress code will be if you are unsure.

People from other countries are welcomed and encouraged to wear their national dress, whether it is a monk's robes, a burqa, a kimono, or a turban. As a tolerant and diverse society, Australians respect cultural differences. However, they resent it when another culture's beliefs are imposed on their way of life.

Surf Safety Tips:

The seemingly calm waters of any Australian beach might look safe, but appearances can be deceptive. In fact, there can be several rip currents operating along the beach at any one time. Sometimes referred to as a "rip", a rip current is a moving current of water that can sometimes be strong or fast flowing. Usually starting near the shoreline, it tends to flow away from the beach. If you are caught in a rip current, it may feel like you are in a fast moving flow of water, like being in a river. Other times you mightn't notice it at all until you are some distance from the shore. For the inexperienced swimmer, being caught in a rip current can induce panic, which can lead to exhaustion and potential drowning. So unless you are proficient at reading the water and spotting rip currents, it's important that you practice the following precautions:

Only swim between the red and yellow flags, particularly if you're not a strong swimmer, and are not familiar with how rips and undercurrents work. You could otherwise be risking your own safety.

If you find yourself caught in a rip, or dangerous current, try your best to stay calm and put your hand up to attract the lifeguards' attention. Their job is to keep their eyes peeled for any trouble in the water, so they will be watching.

If you are caught in a rip, never try to swim towards the shore. This may sound counterintuitive, but heading straight towards the shore means that you will be swimming against the current, which will only exhaust you sooner and increase your chances of drowning. Instead, go with the current and swim parallel to the shore.

Regarding surfing or body boarding, there is an unspoken rule of the water that says the person deepest out has the right of way. However, if someone is heading straight towards you on a board, it's OK to let them know you're there with a wave of your hand. It's either that or ducking your head under the wave very quickly.

Lastly, never swim under the influence of alcohol or drugs. This is no laughing matter. As any sensible Aussie will tell you, the surf can be capricious and erratic. Always remain vigilant while in the water.

Avoidance Practices Of Indigenous Australians:

Australian Aboriginal "avoidance practices" refers to those relationships in traditional Aboriginal society where certain people are required to avoid others in their family or clan as a mark of respect. There are strong protocols around avoiding and averting eye contact.

The traditional Australian Aboriginal requires more personal space than people from other cultures. To intrude on that space, by standing too close or maintaining direct eye contact, represents a lack of respect.

In traditional Aboriginal culture, direct eye contact was a means of asserting power or reprimanding someone. It was, therefore, considered rude or threatening to look another individual in the eye when interacting. Today, eye contact may not always signal a power factor. However, be sensitive to body language. If an Aboriginal is clearly avoiding eye contact, it is a way of showing respect and it may be appropriate for you to look away too.

It is taboo to speak of the dead by name, or through the use of images, reason being that it is too painful for the grieving family. The avoidance period may last anywhere from 12 months to several years. Individuals with the same names are expected to change their name so as not to use the name of the deceased. The deceased person can still be referred to in a roundabout way, such as, "that young man" or "that old lady," but not by their first name.

Today, the avoidance practice includes the publication or dissemination of photography or film footage of the deceased person. Many books and television programs include a warning for Aboriginal and Torres Strait Islanders to "use caution" when viewing a film or reading a book, as it may contain images, voices, or the names of dead persons.

The Aboriginal culture bans a son-in-law from talking directly to his mother-in-law. This includes being in the same room or building at any time, including meal times. They can still communicate via the wife/husband, who remains the main conduit for communication in this relationship.

Brothers and sisters are permitted to play together freely until a boy's initiation, after which avoidance practices come into play.

Safety Precautions:

By and large, Australia is a very safe country to travel to. However, it does have some unsavory areas and is not exempt from crime. Like you would in any major city in the world, find out from the hotel concierge what areas are safe to walk around in, and take the necessary travel safety precautions, particularly in secluded areas and/or after dark.

Loud and rowdy behavior and fights can occur around the popular drinking spots in the major cities, particularly on Friday and Saturday nights. If you are harassed, it's best to ignore those concerned and walk away.

Australia has very strict laws regarding what goods can and can't be brought into Australia, with strong penalties for not declaring prohibited and restricted goods and making false declarations on the Incoming Passenger Card.

[three]
China

Historic Influences:

China's history can be traced back to 50,000BC, when its first inhabitants migrated from Central Asia and India. Originally hunters and gatherers, they began farming rice and raising livestock by 4,000BC, and living in homes and using pottery by 3,000BC. Eventually, the use of the horse and chariot revolutionized their everyday life.

2,000BC saw the advent of the Bronze Age and the use of writing. In 1800BC, the Shang Dynasty conquered most of China and ruled it under one emperor. From this point onwards, China's history became recognized by its dynasties, or family related rulers.

China's position as one of the most advanced cultures in the world remained unrivaled prior to the 19th century. The era of the Zhou

Dynasty (1122BC–256BC) is often looked to as the touchstone of Chinese cultural development. It had a well-developed musical culture, and fine art, folk art, and performance art, which were greatly influenced by the great philosophers, teachers, religious and political figures of the time. The world-renowned Chinese cuisine, also stemmed from the dynasties, when the emperor would host banquets of 100 dishes. Examples of Chinese architecture can be found as far back as 2,000 years ago, with its emphasis on width and symmetry, an important hallmark from palaces to farmhouses.

Despite China's extremely advanced and sophisticated civilization prior to the 19th century, the ruling dynasties that followed missed the Industrial Revolution that occurred in Europe, eventually bringing on the decline of China as a world power. European and Japanese imperialism in the 19th and 20th centuries, coupled with internal weaknesses and civil war, damaged China and its economy, leading to the eventual overthrow of imperial rule.

After the Chinese Civil War ended in 1949, two states calling themselves 'China' emerged: The People's Republic of China, which was established in 1949 and includes mainland China, Hong Kong, and Macau, and the Republic of China, established in 1912, and now commonly known as Taiwan.

While Taiwan's changes in economic policies in the 1950s transformed it into a technology-oriented industrialized developed economy, mainland China under Mao's rule remained underdeveloped and impoverished. Fortunately, reforms led by Deng Xiaoping in the 1970s improved agriculture, industry, and technology, raising living standards once more. While economically frail before 1978, China has once more risen to become one of the world's largest economies and a force to be reckoned with.

So how have the factors that make up China - its complex 5,000 year old history with its diverse range of profound social and cultural influences, a vast geographical area and its 1.3-billion strong population - influenced the psyche of the Chinese people? Over the centuries, China has developed a collectivist culture, meaning that it places greater emphasis on the group rather than the individual. Harmony, loyalty and honor within the group must always be maintained and confrontation avoided at all cost. The achievement of the group - whether a company or the country as a whole - is far more important than those of the individual.

The Chinese Concept of Face:

"He who controls others may be powerful, but he who has mastered himself is mightier still."

– LAO TZU, CHINESE TAOIST, PHILOSOPHER.

When dealing with the Chinese socially or in business, it's vital to understand the concept of "face" and its importance. "Face" can be defined by a person's value, prestige, and standing in the eyes of others. In China's honor-based society, the thought of losing face is the equivalent of social death. To maintain one's "face," one must maintain harmony and avoid conflict. Western societies are considered to have "thick faces" by the Chinese, meaning that Westerners have little regard for non-verbal cues; they tend to be more direct and less polite.

Conflict, to the Chinese, can include disagreements over a point during discussion or directing criticism at someone. Disagreement or criticism must be done gently and tempered with a lot of ego rubbing. You will almost never hear a Chinese utter a direct "no." "Face" in China can also be lost, taken away, or earned through how graciously one gives and receives praise and thanks. This is your cue to be effusive with your praise and thanks when socializing or doing business.

Greeting and Conversation Etiquette:

Names in the Chinese culture follow different conventions to the West. The family name is always written first and the given name second. Chinese people commonly address each other with full names. Family names are never used alone without any salutation. For example, The Chinese athlete, Wang Meng, would be addressed informally by her full name, Wang Meng. In more formal occasions, she would be addressed as Miss Wang, not Miss Meng.

Many Chinese who do business with the West have a Westernized version of their name. Sometimes they just reverse the order of their first and surnames. Many Chinese even adopt a Western name using a combination of the first name, Western name, and surname (e.g., Meng "Lily" Wang). Whenever you're in doubt as to what to call your Chinese friend, simply ask which is the correct way for you to address them.

Attending a dinner with a Chinese group for the first time is an interesting experience for a Western person. You may find yourself fidgeting as your Chinese friends spend an inordinate amount of time engaging in idle chit chat. You may even find some of their questions on your personal life intrusive and, at times, akin to an interrogation. But don't take this personally. It's the Chinese way of finding some common ground. The Chinese use small talk to make up their minds as to whether they like you or not. The more you share of your personal life, which might include family, hobbies, political views, aspirations, the closer you become to them in your relationship.

However, you may draw the line about the disclosure of certain personal information that may cause your Chinese host or colleague discomfort, or for them to judge you harshly (e.g., issues such as single motherhood, homosexuality, and/or divorce). Even though these issues may be widely discussed and accepted in the Western culture, many Chinese are still fairly conservative.

Bowing or nodding is the common greeting for the Chinese. Although handshakes are commonly used between men, men will wait for ladies to offer their hand first before extending theirs. When shaking hands, shake firmly with a smile, good eye contact, and politeness, which are considered expressions of sincerity. If there are several people in the group, start with the most senior, from the nearest to the furthest, and move towards the more junior. Always remove your hat, gloves, or sunglasses while hand-shaking, and never shake hands absent-mindedly or with the left hand. When greeting a crowd, it is common for the Chinese to applaud.

I am often asked how one can work out who is the most senior person in a group of Chinese. It's simple. Start with the eldest and move to the youngest. The Chinese have a very healthy respect for their elders and they are deferred to in any group situation. In a business situation, the eldest member would more than likely be the "boss," or the one with the most experience. Again, when in doubt, ask the person who organized the function to clarify the hierarchy of those attending. As this is important to the Chinese, they will be happy to explain it to you.

Seniority is very important to the Chinese, especially if you are dealing with a state owned or government body, so it is appropriate to address the other party by his or her designation (e.g., Chairman So and So, Director So and So, or Manager So and So). Never address someone by their first name unless you've been given permission to do so. Chinese like to adopt Western nicknames to assist their Western visitors.

The Chinese trust non-verbal messages more than the spoken word as words can have several meanings. They rely heavily on facial expression, tone of voice, and posture to tell them what someone is feeling or thinking, so avoid making unusual or unnecessary facial expressions and gesticulating wildly when conversing with them. For example, frowning while someone is speaking is interpreted as a sign of disagreement to the Chinese.

The Chinese avoid eye contact when they want to give themselves privacy. So staring into another person's eyes, particularly those of a person who is senior to you, shows an invasion of someone's space and disrespect for age or status.

The Chinese are not a tactile people and personal contact must be avoided in conversation, even if it is as innocent a gesture as patting someone on the shoulder. It is even more inappropriate for a man to touch a woman in public, and vice versa.

The Chinese have a strong entrepreneurial spirit and powerful desire to succeed in business. Haggling, bargaining, and making deals is a way of life in China. Remember the concept of "face" and being respectful, even when haggling.

Conversation Taboos:

- Taiwan is still a sore point to many Chinese, so it is best to avoid mentioning Taiwan as an independent state or a country.

- When discussing the Chinese leaders, you may condemn Mao Tse Tung but avoid criticizing Deng Xiaoping.

- The other topics that won't score you any credit with the Chinese is praising the Japanese, and praising Shanghai in front of people from Beijing and vice versa. There is a rivalry that exists between the two cities.

- The Chinese frequently consult the stars, the *I Ching*, and principles of Feng Shui before making any important personal or business decisions. Scoffing at, or making fun of, these beliefs is considered a major *faux pas*.

Appropriate Social Behavior:

You will find out soon enough that the Chinese concept of personal space is not the same as in the West, so avoid backing away if the person you are conversing with seems to be getting a little too close for your comfort. They are merely trying to establish some sort of rapport. Similarly, when you feel someone pushing and shoving you from behind while you're waiting in line for a train or bus in Hong Kong or China, resist the temptation to push back or verbally abuse anyone. This is normal behavior with the Chinese, so take it in your stride.

The Chinese are extremely punctual, so being on time for social invitations, even a little earlier for a business meeting, is vital.

When giving out anything, whether they be gifts, business cards, or brochures, make sure that you start with the most senior person before moving down the line, ensuring that both your hands are stretched out with the item, and positioning the item so that it is facing the recipient in the correct manner.

Avoid any acts that involve the mouth, as it is considered unhygienic (e.g., putting your hand in your mouth, biting your nails, and removing food from your teeth).

Gift Giving Etiquette:

The concept of *Gei MianZi*, or giving due respect, is very important in China, particularly in business. It's all about giving the appropriate respect according to rank and seniority. This means buying better gifts for people of seniority than those of a lower, or more junior, status. Gifts should be accepted graciously and with both hands.

Gifts from the West were especially appreciated in China in the "old" days. Today, however, practically everything that is sold in the West is made in China, so the gifts no longer have the appeal they once had. Having said that, gifts are always appreciated, especially in the smaller cities or towns, and continue to play an important part in any relationship with the Chinese. Try giving the gift of something special that is unique from your country or culture.

The most common events for presenting a gift are at festivals, weddings, and birthdays. A bouquet of flowers, perfumes, scarves, quality writing pens, or a seasonal product are all great gift ideas, with attention paid in wrapping the gift beautifully, showing that there has been thought entered into the gift and the recipient. Toys or candies are appropriate gifts to give your host's children if you are invited for a meal in someone's home.

Flowers are given for personal occasions rather than business, but they can get a bit tricky, as each type of flower has a certain significance for the Chinese. Here are some interpretations:

- Jonquils or a Chinese evergreen symbolize health and long life, so these are ideal for sending to the elderly on their birthdays.

- Giving roses and lilies are appropriate as a romantic gesture, so unless romance is your intention, you may want to avoid giving these to your host.

- Chinese roses, red palms, golden rod, and baby's-breath are good flowers for a friend's birthday as they symbolize good prospects during the best years of one's life.

- Roses, lilies, tulips, common freesia, African chrysanthemums, red palms, and birds of paradise flowers are good for congratulating friends on their wedding.

- When paying visits to relatives and friends during festivals, you should send lucky grass, lilies and tulips, which symbolize happiness and luck.

- It is appropriate to send orchids, narcissus, callas lilies and sword lilies to a sick or convalescing person.

- Avoid sending a potted flower or plant to a sick person as they can symbolize incompletely cured illnesses.

- Strongly scented or brightly colored flowers are not ideal gifts for a sick person either, as the former may harm the sick by causing throat irritations, while the latter may mentally stimulate the sick too much when they need to rest.

The following gifts and/or colors are associated with death and should not be given: clocks, straw sandals, anything that has a stork or crane, handkerchiefs, anything white, blue or black. Never present elderly Chinese with toys or watches, or ill people with medicines.

The most generous gift that you can give to a Chinese is to invite them and their family to a banquet, which leads us onto the next topic.

Dining Etiquette:

The Chinese love to eat, and love nothing more than a good banquet. Rule of thumb is to always arrive on time, or slightly earlier; bring your host a gift, and be seated only when invited to do so. It is always wise to remember that there is an elaborate seating arrangement for a Chinese meal, with host and guests seated according to age and seniority, so it's always best to wait for your host to seat you. Eating or drinking before your host is considered very bad manners.

Apart from soup, all delicacies should be eaten with chopsticks. If you haven't mastered the art, I strongly suggest that you do a crash course prior to your trip to China, along with the etiquette that goes with it. Here are some things to remember:

- Hold your chopstick closer to the thicker end at the top, not in the middle or all the way towards the front (slimmer end).

- Never stick your chopsticks into your food, and especially not into the rice. The practice of sticking chopsticks into the rice is reserved for funerals, when rice is placed at the altar.

- Remember that your chopsticks are not a conductor's baton or magic wand that you wave around in the air while speaking, nor is it something that you spear food with, move bowls and plates around with, or drum on the tables.

- Passing food from your set of chopsticks to another's is a no-no, as this too is a funeral practice.

- When you're serving yourself food from shared dishes, use the opposite end of your chopsticks (thicker end) to move some food from the shared plates onto your own if you have not already eaten from your chopsticks. Otherwise, use the serving chopsticks that may be provided for that purpose.

- Do not drop your chopsticks, as it is considered bad luck.

It is polite to taste all the dishes that you are offered by the host, but keep in mind that there will be several courses on offer, so you may want to pace yourself. Do not eat all of your meal. If you eat all of your meal, the Chinese will assume you did not receive enough food and are still hungry.

The one who sits closest to the teapot or wine bottle should pour for others from the most senior to the junior. If someone else fills your cup or glass, receive the cup with both hands and respond with thanks.

Toasts are characteristic of Chinese dining, particularly during formal business dinners, which can drag on for quite some time. Expect there to be lots of talk, some karaoke, and drinking contests. If the business partnership is only new, you are unlikely to be invited to further after-dinner entertainment. Your host pays for all bills on the night, including all entertainment. It is impolite to fight for the bill or worse, split the bill. Similarly, if you are the host for the night, or when reciprocating back in your own country, you are expected to pick up all expenses on the night.

Drinking Etiquette:

The Chinese are big drinkers, especially in northern and western China. No matter if it is lunch or dinner, as long as a meal is being hosted, there will be alcohol. Chinese traditional wine is the favorite alcoholic beverage of choice in China, particularly for males, followed by red wine, then beer.

Traditional Chinese wine is usually warmed before drinking. But tread carefully here, as it is more rocket fuel than liquor. With an alcohol concentration of as much as 60%, no matter how good a drinker you may think you are, never challenge a Chinese into a drinking contest.

Here's a tip for you if you don't drink: It is often seen as rude not to take part in drinking with the Chinese in a formal dinner. If you don't like the idea of getting drunk, or don't want to drink at all, either claim to be a non-drinker or plead medical grounds as an excuse. Better yet, bring a partner who can drink on your behalf.

Dressing Etiquette:

Remember that the Chinese are very conservative and frown on women who display too much skin. Subtle dress colors or all black are more appropriate than bright colors. When dressing casually, jeans are acceptable so long as they are neat. When attending an official function or meeting, avoid sleeveless and short-sleeved dresses, shirts, and jeans.

Safety Precautions:

As you would when traveling to other countries, always exercise common sense and caution, and look out for suspicious behavior.

Always monitor political developments in China, particularly if traveling to Tibet, due to the risk of civil unrest. You should not attempt to travel to Tibet without permission from the Chinese authorities.

The Chinese authorities have put in place more stringent requirements for visa issue. Always check with the nearest Embassy or Consulate of China for detailed information well in advance of your intended travel date.

If traveling to Hong Kong, take note that the typhoon season is between May and October. You should keep informed of regional weather forecasts and plan accordingly.

[f o u r]

France

Historic Influences:

French civilization has been ruled by a number of great dynasties, from the Bourbons and Valois to the Capetians, molding
the country to become one of the greatest civilizations in the
world. Extremely rich and populated, France had no shortage of
dangerous neighbors eagerly awaiting any opportunity to take the
country over: the Germans, English, Vikings, and the Arabs. As a
result, the policy of all French rulers, from the Franc kings to the
Sun King, Louis XIV, and Napoleon, was to develop a strong state
that would be able to withstand the onslaught of foreign invaders.
At the peak of its power, France was indeed the most powerful
nation in Europe.

With a cultural tradition that was controlled by the nobility, and
huge resources allocated to art and pleasure for the glory of God

and King, it is little wonder that the French have been known throughout history as the world's arbiters of taste. In fact, Louis XIV almost singlehandedly created fashion and style as we know it today.

Greeting & Conversation Etiquette:

With a reputation that dates back to their monarchial tradition where the court gathered the brightest minds of the realm, the French are considered to be the world's best conversationalists. And with all their questioning and probing, they seem to treat all discussion as an intellectual exercise. While their conversational manner can seem very straightforward, it has many complexities.

While it's acceptable in Anglo-Saxon countries for people to greet a group with a generic, "Hi, everyone, how are you?" followed by a group wave, the French would consider this manner of greeting uneducated and vulgar. Preferring more formality with their greetings, particularly with new acquaintances, they greet each and every person individually, even when in a group, and the same goes when it's time to say goodbye. And yes, that can take a while. The acceptable greeting in France is *bonjour* or *bonsoir* (good morning or good evening) to each person, followed by the honorific title of *Monsieur* or *Madame* if you do not know him or her well. *Au revoir'* (goodbye) is used when saying goodbye.

The French reserve first names for family and close friends, so wait until invited before using someone's first name. The titles *Monsieur* and *Madame* are used as a sign of respect, and *Mademoiselle* is reserved for young girls or people considered to be of lesser importance, such as a waitress or coat-check girl. You can be 19 years of age and still be called *Madame* by a maître d' at a formal restaurant.

Friends may greet each other with a *bonjour* or *bonsoir* and a *bisou*, or air-kiss on the side of each cheek, once on the left cheek and once on the right. It is women that instigate the *bisou*, and the men follow suit. If you don't know someone well, then a simple *bonjour* without the *bisou* is more than sufficient.

Salut (the equivalent of ciao in Italy) can also be used between close friends, pronounced "sal-ooh." When saying goodbye, repeat the same process as when you arrived, saying *salut, à plus tard, à bientôt,* or *au revoir* – meaning "goodbye" or "until next time."

If you do not speak French, an apology for not knowing the language may help in developing a relationship. Nevertheless, try to attempt a few key phrases in French, as it will always be appreciated. The French are polite enough to revert back to English if they see that you are struggling.

The French tend to stand close when speaking with each other, with touching and patting of the arms and shoulders common-place in the French social etiquette, even in business. Eye contact is important as long as it isn't too obtrusive.

The French prefer to speak in hushed tones, even in the midst of a heated debate. Speaking too loudly or gesticulating wildly is considered vulgar. You can spot if you are speaking too loudly if someone who is not in your company is trying to listen in on your conversation.

Beware the French smile. Never assume it is a greeting or sign of approval. Rather, look for the subtle hints and unspoken words. If the smile is not accompanied by verbal approval, or even a polite phrase, then it may well signal disapproval.

Discussions are likely to get intense, with disagreements not only permitted but also encouraged. Keep the discussions good-natured, and whatever you do, never lose your cool.

The French are not interested in the weather, your new car, your vacation, or the latest deal that you struck at work. They'd rather exercise their brains and conversation skills by talking about your country, history, and politics. Other welcome topics of conversation include French cuisine, art, music, and philosophy. However, be cautious about displaying too much of an expertise on a topic as you run the risk of alienating some of the participants, a faux pas in French conversational ethics.

Unlike the United States, wealth has never been an accepted measure for social status in France, so don't bother trying to impress the French with how much money you make or how much you have. What does impress them is what university you went to, your clever conversation and wit, your knowledge on culture, or with whom you socialize.

When speaking with someone over the telephone, introduce yourself first and always apologize for disturbing the household if you happen to call at mealtimes.

Conversation Taboos:

- The French take the art of conversation very seriously, so avoid exaggerated claims. Only express opinions on subjects that you know well. Otherwise, practice the art of active listening.

- It is considered a major *faux pas* to ask a new acquaintance what he or she does for a living, as the job title will often give an indication of his salary. It's safer to stick to discussions of food and drink.

- Talks about sex can get earthy in France, but until you've figured out how to navigate this particular topic of conversation, it's best to avoid it altogether.

- Lastly, never ever criticize Napoleon.

Appropriate Social Behavior:

A great source of frustration for Westerners living in France, particularly in Paris, is that the French take their time in deciding if they want to socialize with you. So don't be disappointed if you're not invited to a social gathering straight away. Likewise, they may find it embarrassing if you invited them for a lunch or dinner before they've gotten to know you well enough.

Management hierarchy is very important to the French, so don't make the mistake of crossing hierarchy lines when dealing with a public official, unless you're certain that it's accepted.

If you're in an office environment, forget about appearing like a hard worker by skipping lunch and coffee breaks. Lunch and coffee breaks are important to the French, and they will just think you're strange if you skip them.

Although the French are into good grooming, never brush your hair, primp, or apply make-up in public. This is best saved for the privacy of a washroom or your hotel room.

People from Anglo-Saxon cultures love to make non-verbal gestures with their hands, particularly the OK sign of the circle made with the thumb and forefinger. However in France, it means that the other person is a big, fat "zero." So if you want to show your approval, raise your thumb instead. When in doubt, avoid making any gestures with your hands or fingers. Never make the mistake of slapping an open palm over a closed fist if you want to emphasize a point. This is considered really rude in France. And God forbid that you should snap your fingers at anyone. Unless you're putting your hand out and snapping your fingers to hail a taxi, this gesture is considered insulting.

Don't be disheartened if you happen to smile at someone on the street and find that they don't smile back. The French only smile at people that they know.

Poise and good posture are essential to the French, therefore to slouch or put your hands in your pockets when speaking with anyone is seen as poor form. And lastly, although you may think that chewing gum freshens the breath, aids in digestion, and generally improves the physique (I have yet to be convinced), chewing gum in public in France is considered vulgar.

Gift Giving Etiquette:

The French appreciate the good things in life, so if you are attending a dinner invitation and are bringing a gift for the host - wine, flowers, chocolate - make sure that it is of the highest quality that you can afford. Gift giving is always done with discretion, and usually opened when received.

When giving flowers, never give lilies or chrysanthemums (considered funeral flowers), red carnations (considered bad luck), or any white flowers (associated with weddings). Flowers should also be given in odd numbers but not in a bouquet of 13, which is considered unlucky.

When invited to a large dinner party, especially in Paris, it is customary to send flowers to your host in the morning of the occasion, so that he or she can display the arrangement that evening when the guests arrive.

Dining Etiquette:

Social gatherings in France can be nerve wracking for those who come from a more relaxed and casual culture. However, they need not be a social minefield. You can start by being punctual, arriving no more than 10 minutes late, and bring a small gift for your host. If you expect to be delayed, telephone immediately and offer an explanation.

If there is a seating plan, you may be directed to a particular seat on the dining table. Only begin eating after the hostess has said *bon appétit*.

Eating in France is done Continental style, which means that the fork is held in the left hand and the knife in the right. Refrain from resting your elbows on the table. Hands should be visible and not on your lap.

If you have not finished eating, cross your knife and fork on your plate with the fork over the knife. Finish everything on your plate, as leaving food on the plate signifies that you did not enjoy your meal. When you have finished eating, place your knife and fork together on the bottom right hand side of your plate. Leave your wineglass nearly full if you do not want your wine glass refilled.

The French eat salad quite delicately, so cutting up a salad with a knife and fork, or picking up the lettuce with your hand, is a real no-no. Rather, fold the lettuce on to your fork before bringing it to your mouth.

Always peel and slice fruit before eating it with your knife and fork. Never pick it up with your fingers and take a big bite out of it, juices dripping down your chin and arm.

Dressing Etiquette:

The French tend to judge people by the way they dress, a behavior that stems from the days of the French court. With style and quality being as important as the correct dress code for the occasion, the French version of "casual" is not as relaxed as in many Western countries. To be on the safe side, just do as the French do: wear classically cut fashion and good basics in styles that suit you, in the very best quality that you can afford.

On invitations, the terms *smoking exigé/tenue de soirée* means formal dress, which translates to black tie for men and full evening dress for women. *Tenue de ville* means informal dress. And while French dress habits have become more casual over the years, an informal dress code stipulated on a lunch or dinner invitation does not mean that you will be well received if you turn up in a T-shirt and scruffy jeans. Jeans that are worn to the office or to dinner in France will more than likely be a designer label, worn with a well-cut designer jacket and clever accessorizing.

Never dress for comfort at the expense of style in France. This means that wearing sneakers, baseball caps, tracksuit pants, shorts, and flip-flops are a no-no, unless you're headed to the gym or are at the beach. Shorts, halter tops, and revealing outfits are inappropriate for anywhere other than the beach, and certainly never when sightseeing and visiting churches and cathedrals. Churches are places of worship and revealing plenty of skin is a definite sign of disrespect.

In France, less is more. Ostentatious wealth has never been an accepted measure for social status, so avoid wearing showy jewelry and accessories as a way to impress the French. They will consider this boring and in poor taste. Discreet, elegant, and "clever" accessories are more their style.

Make-up should always be understated, with the emphasis on the glow of the complexion. The look is clean, natural, and fresh, not dramatic or overly painted, even though the lips may be a bold scarlet. Hairstyles must never be overdone or complex.

Safety Precautions:

The nature of crime in France, particularly Paris, is by and large, petty theft. Bag snatching, pick-pocketing, passport theft, and theft from cars is common, particularly around major tourist attractions, like the Louvre and Eiffel Tower, railway stations, airports, and bus terminals, with the petty crime rate rising in the busy tourist season.

Keep your wits about you at all times, and be vigilant with your belongings, especially your passport. Thieves will often create a diversion (e.g., pretending to ask for directions, throwing items on the floor or on their intended victim) and rob people when their attention is diverted. Pick-pocketing, bag snatching and bag slashing, are common.

five

Germany

"An appeal to fear never finds echo in German hearts."

– OTTO VON BISMARCK, GERMAN STATESMAN.

Historic Influences:

Up until 1871, Europe's German-speaking territories were divided into several hundred kingdoms, principalities, duchies, fiefdoms and independent cities and towns. Finding the right form of statehood for the German speaking lands, and which form of government provides the most peace and stability, has defined most of German history. The history of many independent policies, as opposed to a centralized one, is the basis for the decentralized nature of German political and cultural life that lasts to this day.

Unfortunately, German culture has long suffered the ignoble reputation of being purist and xenophobic (meaning fearful of foreigners). This cultural characteristic would have stemmed from a time in the early 19th century, the period between the French Revolution and World War I, when German society venerated their Teutonic bloodlines and rejected any perceived intrusion of any other culture. Although this mindset may have been a strong characteristic of the national psyche at the time, it most certainly isn't the case today.

Having said that, certain traits of Germany's mono-cultural roots still remain, particularly with the older and more conservative members of the population. An entrenched institutional hierarchy still exists, which requires quite a bit of formality. But formality does not equal abruptness or arrogance. The Germans are an extremely polite and friendly people who take immense pride in their efficiency.

Germany has one of the highest levels of education, technological advancement, and economic productivity in the world. While German may be the language commonly spoken in Germany, contemporary Germany consists of people hailing from mixed ethnic backgrounds, with the Turkish people forming the largest group at 2.4%, and other foreign residents from Eastern and Western Europe making up 9% of the population. Most foreign residents do not hold German citizenship, despite being born and raised in Germany. This is due to Germany's restrictive citizenship laws. Having said that, the German Government introduced some citizenship and immigration law reforms in 2002, which has given more foreigners the freedom to naturalize.

Greeting & Conversation Etiquette:

"Whenever the literary German dives into a sentence, that is the last you are going to see of him until he emerges on the other side of the Atlantic with his verb in his mouth."

– MARK TWAIN, AMERICAN AUTHOR AND HUMORIST.

Germans are basically a formal people who are not big on "small talk" with strangers. While the art of conversation between strangers evolved out of the need to bridge considerable cultural gaps between people in countries like the United States and Australia, Germany's largely non-immigration mono-cultural background presented little need to entertain people outside of their own ethnic group.

Due to this particular character trait, do not be surprised if your German host fails to go out of their way to introduce you to an established group straight away in order to make you "feel welcome." Whether it be in an office, social gathering, or new neighborhood, unless you are specifically invited to join the group, you will need to instigate any introductions yourself. Be warned that your attempts at introducing yourself to an established group may be met with some awkwardness. In addition to that, you'll more than likely have to work hard at keeping the conversation going.

Firm, brief handshakes and a greeting with each person in a group is standard at the time of arrival and departure in both business and social relationships in Germany. As in France, a general group wave will not be appreciated. Eye contact during introductions is direct, and should be maintained as long as the person is addressing you. Hugging and kissing on both cheeks are only common among good friends and family members.

German formality and entrenched institutional hierarchy dictates the order of how people address each other. First names are usually reserved for family members, as well as friends and close colleagues. It's common in Germany for colleagues who have worked together for years to remain on a formal, last name basis. The terms *Herr* or *Frau* (Mr and Mrs), followed by the surname, is the accepted way to address anyone. *Fräulein* (Miss) is a term that has become out of fashion. Once a girl comes of age, she is normally addressed as *Frau* in public.

"Dr" can be a medical or academic title in Germany, and is often used as part of their names in documentation. When addressing a medical doctor, always add the *Herr or Frau before Doktor* (e.g., *Herr Doktor Meyer*). If you are going to meet a professor, address him/her as *Herr or Frau Professor.*

General rule of thumb would be to always use *"sie"* (more formal version of "you"), especially with a person of seniority, unless someone invites you to use *"Du,"* the more casual version.

When shopping, it's common courtesy in Germany to say *guten tag* ("hello") to the shop assistant when entering a store, and *vielen dank, auf Wiedersehen* ("thank you, goodbye") when leaving. Hallo is also often used to get someone's attention in Germany, much like "excuse me." Like the French, greeting strangers on the street is not the usual practice in Germany, so don't expect a return greeting despite direct eye contact.

Unlike the United States, when you ask *Wie geht es Ihnen?* ("How are you?"), Germans will take this as a literal question that expects a literal answer. Then they might proceed to give you a very detailed response, including why they are not doing so well at that moment. It's a better idea to refrain from using this casual greeting, as many will find it overly familiar. Similarly, giving compliments is not part of German social protocol and can often be viewed with suspicion.

When picking up the phone to answer a call, it is expected for you to identify yourself to the caller with your last name. A simple "hello" can throw the caller off, leading him or her to ask, "with whom am I speaking to?"

Germans are very straightforward and direct in conversation, especially with their disagreement and criticism. They have no problem saying "no," "I can't," or "this is impossible" if that is exactly what they mean. Although this might be confronting if you come from an Asian or Mediterranean culture, the German sees this as a statement based on an objective truth. The value to a German lies in pointing out a mistake to someone so that it can be corrected. Similarly, it is acceptable to ask for clarification if there is anything that you do not understand, as it is part of the German's normal communication behavior to openly ask for clarification.

Most Germans will assume that you are from a part of the world based on how you look. For example, if you were born and raised in the United States or Australia, but have obvious Mediterranean or Asian looks, be prepared for questioning from strangers that attempt to establish where you are "really" from. Take this in the spirit that it is given and avoid getting offended. Germans really do have a genuine fascination and curiosity for bloodlines and ethnicity.

Germans are forceful when it comes to discussions, often continuing to speak and raising the volume of their voices to avoid being interrupted by someone else; interruptions are an effective tactic for holding the floor and being heard. It's never considered good form to get emotional or lose one's cool during discussion. The only time a German allows himself to get emotional is if their sense of order and routine becomes challenged. But despite being so direct, Germans are sensitive to their own public "face," so beware of unintentionally saying or doing anything to embarrass Germans publicly.

Avoid overly dramatic, emotional, or flowery communication styles, which can make Germans cautious and distrustful. Germans are intensely analytical thinkers, requiring lots of facts and examples. They will not relate to an overly emotional or dramatic style of communication. When presenting an idea or concept to a German, tone down the "hype" and provide lots of data, logical solutions, and concrete examples. Keep any personal feelings and relationships out of any business negotiations. At the end of a presentation or lively discussion, Germans will often signal their approval or thanks by gently rapping their knuckles on the tabletop instead of applauding.

Be careful with using humor in conversation as German humor is totally different to that from other Anglo-Saxon nations. Sarcasm and irony are concepts that Germans find hard to grasp as they take whatever is said quite literally. If you said anything outrageous with a serious face, they will not get the joke as an Englishman or Australian would. In fact, the Germans will more than likely try to correct you if your statement sounds ridiculous or absurd.

Welcome topics of conversation include the following: sports (particularly soccer or football), travel, current events/ politics (if you are knowledgeable on the topic), experiences and travels in Germany and other parts of Europe, beer and various brews.

Conversation Taboos:

- Germans are a private people who have clear boundaries between work and their personal life. Unlike the Spaniards, it is not the done thing in a professional environment to ask your colleague about their family or children. And discussing salary or how much someone makes is considered in bad taste and highly intrusive.

- The topic of World War II is a very sensitive one. The Germans have erected many museums, exhibitions and memorials honoring those who suffered in the war and in the Holocaust, and are aware of the war crimes committed at the time. Asking what someone's grandfather did in the war, or if their family was aware of what was going on, implies judgment and is a definite conversation taboo in Germany, as is the subject of nationalism.

Here is what Kathrin Luty, Founder of Web Design That Sells, and German born and bred, had to say:

"[As a German] I have taken enough abuse for [the war] over the years, believe me, to the point of people throwing stones at us on a beach in England when we were 16, the same age as the throwers. I have no problem entering into a quality discussion about [the war], but frankly, I'm getting quite bored talking about it. When I was working as a vet in England ... I actually stopped telling people [that] I was German."

Appropriate Social Behavior:

Never underestimate the importance of punctuality in the German culture. Arriving even five to ten minutes later than the appointed time is perceived as late. Half an hour late would be considered a very serious *faux pas*. If you must be late for any reason, it's important that you call and notify the person who is expecting you and give a plausible explanation for the delay. Casually changing the time and place of an appointment is not appreciated. If you must change or cancel appointments, try to give at least 24 hours notice and offer a plausible explanation.

Germans need more time than most cultures to form relationships on a personal level. The concept of "mingling" doesn't really exist in the German culture. Parties are generally considered opportunities for good friends to "hang out." They are rarely seen as a chance to meet new people. So if you arrive at a party where you know only the host and one or two other acquaintances, be prepared to find yourself alone with a drink in your hand for a large part of the evening. The plus side to this attitude is that you don't have to go out of your way at the beginning of a relationship with a German either, as they wouldn't expect it of you.

Professional rank and status in Germany are largely determined by the individual's achievements. Therefore, if you come from a highly hierarchical culture, be prepared for a woman or much younger person to have the highest rank in the German group you will be dealing with.

Flexibility and spontaneity are not prominent traits in the German social or business culture. The older the institution or person, the more conservative and slow-moving they will be. It's not a good idea to challenge rules and traditional authority. Breaking the rules in German society is taken very seriously. However, despite the high value of rules and social order in most aspects of public life in Germany, pushing, shoving, and other displays of impatience in line-ups and queues are not uncommon.

Gift Giving Etiquette:

Foreign guests are not usually invited into a German home unless a close friendship already exists. Should you have the opportunity to be invited to a dinner in a German home, a small gift for your host is considered polite. Avoid selecting anything that is obviously expensive, as this may make your host feel obligated and awkward, and your intentions misinterpreted. Fine chocolates and flowers are an appropriate gift for a dinner invitation. Ask the florist to wrap the flowers especially as a gift.

Other appropriate gifts include imported liquor, wines of excellent vintages from your home country, coffee table books, and good quality handicrafts that are representative of your country. An elegant silk scarf is a great gift idea for the lady of the house. A local food specialty of your home country makes an interesting gift too, but keep in mind that German tastes are generally on the conservative side, so flavors that are too exotic may not be appreciated. Clothing, perfumes, and other toiletries are considered too personal to be appropriate gifts. Avoid bringing beer as a gift in Germany. It's the equivalent of bringing ice to Eskimos.

Flowers to avoid as gifts are red roses, lilies, and heather in a bouquet. Red roses are for lovers, lilies are used in funerals, and heather is planted in cemeteries.

Dining Etiquette:

Germans make a very clear distinction between business and personal relationships, so unless a close personal relationship already exists between business partners and a foreign guest, guests should not expect to be invited into private homes for dinner to meet the family, or to be shown effusive hospitality straight away. If you are invited to a home for a meal, more often than not it will be a sit-down dinner in the evening. A more common invitation is for afternoon *Kaffee trinken,* which roughly means "for coffee and cake."

Dinner is usually served between 7:00pm and 8:30pm in most German homes. This is also the customary time for dinner parties to begin. Sit-down dinner parties begin punctually, so if you must be late for any reason, it's important that you call and notify your hosts, giving a plausible explanation for the delay. Dinner parties usually end at about midnight.

German cuisine is traditionally heavy on the meats, so if you are vegetarian or have any dietary restrictions, let your host know directly, politely, and well in advance. Remaining silent and bringing the problem up with the host when you arrive is not only unnecessary, it will result in your host becoming annoyed with you for disrupting their catering plans.

Eating in Germany is done Continental style, using a knife and fork. There will often be many additional pieces of cutlery on the table, such as for appetizers, buttering bread, dessert, etc. If you are unsure of which utensil to use, the best policy is to start from the outside and work your way in, course by course. Better yet, watch what everyone else does.

Eating with only one hand with the other hand placed on one's lap under the table, as is often done in the United States, is not considered sophisticated table etiquette. Do not lean over your plate when eating. Instead, remain relatively upright, leaning only slightly forward as you bring your fork or spoon towards your mouth. If you are familiar with French table etiquette you won't have any problems in Germany.

Always wait to be told where to sit by your German host during any dinner party. Traditionally, the most honored position is at the head of the table, with individuals of the greatest importance seated first to the left and then to the right of the head of the table. Do not expect to be served by your host or fellow diners, even if you are the honored guest at the dinner. Germans do not generally serve other people. Plates of food are passed around the table and each person takes what, and how much, he or she wants. It is customary for the host to say *Guten Appetit* ("Enjoy your meal!") before anyone takes the first bite.

When eating or drinking soup, refrain from making audible slurping sounds. Although acceptable in Asia, this is considered very bad table manners not only in Germany but throughout Europe.

If you do not want any more food or drink, say so politely. Germans will not ask again, as they always expect you to express your personal wishes openly and directly. Avoid leaving significant portions of food on your plate, as this may suggest to your host that you find something wrong with it.

Your German host will often ask his guests if they would like more to drink. In the case of wine, the host usually does the pouring. However, if you are seated at a large table, it's perfectly normal to pass the wine bottle to the person who wants it.

When the meal is finished, the knife and fork are laid parallel to each other across the right side of the plate. It will be taken as a signal to your host, or waiter at a restaurant, that your dishes can be cleared away.

Very few foods in Germany are intended to be eaten with the hands. Americans are often surprised to find that even pizzas are eaten with a knife and fork in Germany, unless sold by the piece to go.

With regards to smoking after a meal, ask permission before lighting up, unless people around you are already smoking. It's considered polite to offer cigarettes to those in your company.

Send a hand-written thank you card to your hosts for their invitation when you get home. Never thank your host via email or a text message on your cell phone as this would be considered the height of rudeness.

Even if you are staying for several days, do not expect your German friends to take you out every evening for meals or keep you entertained. They will always assume that you will want time to yourself since this is also a high priority for them in their culture. If you are hosting German guests, it isn't necessary for you to arrange a full program for them either, as they will want to have time for themselves.

Regarding a lunch or dinner invitation at a restaurant, the person who extends the invitation is the person who pays. In fact, the guest should not even offer to pay, so don't start making any dramatic or persistent efforts to obtain the bill or even share the costs. This will only create confusion and embarrassment for your host. And because Germans take whatever you say quite literally, if you fight hard enough for the bill, you could end up paying for the lot.

If a German colleague or friend suggests that you go out to get something to eat, this should not to be taken as an invitation. At the more informal restaurants, you may be asked if you would mind sharing a table with other patrons if there are no free tables available. Do not feel obligated to socialize with the other people at the table if you end up sharing a table. At the end of the meal, the waiter will ask you and your companion if the total should be *zusammen* ("in one bill") or *getrennt* ("separate bills"). Unless you have been explicitly invited, you can expect to pay separately, in which case the waiter will add together what you have just eaten and you will pay him directly at the table.

Non-smoking sections in restaurants are still uncommon in most European countries, so refrain from exercising your non-smoker rights too vocally here. This will be met with indignation and very little public support.

Drinking Etiquette:

The Germans are justifiably proud of their long-standing beer heritage, and few other products in Germany are viewed with as much emotion. While the Germans will accept price increases on all other goods, the price of beer always remains stable. Raising it would result in a national riot.

Having a drink with Germans means toasting, and lots of it. When joining a group for drinks, it is customary for everyone in the group to wait until everybody has received their glass before jointly toasting the first drink together. When toasting with wine, *Zum Wohl* is used, and with beer, *Prost,* both meaning "good health." When making a toast, it is important to maintain direct eye contact from the time the glass is raised, clinking glasses with each person, until it is placed back on the table.

When visiting a bar, find a seat and wait for a waiter or waitress to approach you. You will then be given a beer-mat (decker) where your drinks will be marked, after which you will be expected to settle-up your order at the end of the evening. If you move to another table, your waiter or waitress may ask you to settle your bill immediately to avoid confusion later on.

Dressing Etiquette:

German men and women tend to "dress up" more, even when doing routine things such as walking the dog or going to the bank and supermarket. The preferred style for German women consists of beautifully tailored classical pieces in muted colors, teamed with silk scarves and exquisite shoes and handbag. Although designer jeans and a tailored jacket is quite normal weekend wear for adult men and women, it is not appropriate for an evening meal at an upscale restaurant or an invitation in someone's home.

If you receive an invitation stating "informal" dress, never assume that you will be welcome in a T-shirt and jeans. Informal more often than not means tastefully coordinated clothes. An invitation that states "formal" dress usually means formal evening wear. For women, this means cocktail wear or an evening gown, depending on the occasion.

Similarly to France, avoid wearing sweat shirts and sweat pants, and other casual sporting dress in Germany. They are only seen on teenagers, students, or at the gym. Women should avoid excessively ornate jewelry, as displays of affluence in Germany are seen as poor taste.

Driving Etiquette:

The population density of Germany, and a culture that includes endless rules and regulations, seem to have produced an aggressive "driving culture" on Germany's autobahns. The absence of speed limits plus German automotive engineering doesn't help the situation either. Tailgating is common, especially on the left lane, where etiquette dictates that slower vehicles give way immediately by moving to the right lane. Be prepared for much "chasing" and maneuvering, which can make driving very stressful.

Meanwhile, back in the cities, pedestrians are expected to wait patiently on the curb until the light turns green before crossing the street. As German drivers expect everyone to follow the rules, jaywalking will be met with a reprimand or a honk of the horn. However, in a country where it is very common for people to walk or cycle everywhere, German drivers are cautious with pedestrians and cyclists.

Safety Precautions:

Germany has a low incidence of violent crime. As with all major towns and cities in Europe, street crime does occur, including pick-pocketing and theft from unattended vehicles.

Extremist youth groups, particularly in urban areas and in states of the former East Germany, have harassed or attacked individuals because they appear foreign, so exercise caution when visiting these areas.

Six

Great Britain

> "The farther backward you can look, the farther forward you are likely to see."
>
> **— WINSTON CHURCHILL, BRITISH POLITICIAN AND STATESMAN**

Historic Influences:

In the 1920s, the British Empire was the foremost global power and the largest empire in world history, holding sway over approximately one-quarter of the world's population. Its culture, industrial, political, and linguistic legacy on the rest of the world remains unsurpassed.

The British monarchy is the constitutional monarchy of the United Kingdom and its overseas territories. Since 1927, the official description of the nation that lies off the northwest coast of continental Europe has been the United Kingdom of Great Britain and Northern Ireland. Great Britain consists of three distinct entities: England, Scotland, and Wales. For most of the global population, Great Britain is simply "England" and its people are "English" or just "British."

With a history firmly entrenched in the monarchy for more than a thousand years, British society became divided into three main groups of classes: the Upper Class, which includes the oldest families and titled aristocrats with inherited wealth, the Middle Class, made up of professionals, business people, industrialists, doctors and lawyers, and the Working Class, people in agriculture, mining, store workers, and factory workers. Although features of its class-ridden society still remain, multiculturalism and a changing economy in Great Britain are gradually eroding the British class system.

Greeting and Conversation Etiquette:

"We are masters of the unsaid words, but slaves of those we let slip out."

– WINSTON CHURCHILL, BRITISH POLITICIAN AND STATESMAN.

The Brits are obsessive about maintaining and respecting personal space, which explains why they have a certain reserve when engaging in conversation, which is controlled and discreet at all times. The British never gesticulate wildly, make dramatic facial expressions, or raise their voices when speaking.

When meeting an Englishman or woman for the first time, it's best that you simply shake hands with them and use the phrase "How do you do?" or "Pleased to meet you". Always use the title Mr, Mrs, Dr, Professor, Sir, followed by the surname when addressing someone you have just met. Always wait to be invited before using someone's first name. And while Dale Carnegie said that a person's name is to that person the sweetest and most important sound in the world, the British beg to differ. They find the American habit of constantly repeating someone's name in the course of the conversation cloying and overly familiar.

Unlike people from the Mediterranean, the British are not big on social kissing, hugging, or backslapping. They reserve this behavior for family members and very close friends. Regarding personal space, the British give each other a much wider berth than in the Middle East, Asia, or Spain. You can just picture the scenario, can't you? The Spaniard conversing with an Englishman, grabbing arms and patting shoulders, gesticulating wildly, speaking animatedly, while the Englishman closes in on himself in discomfort, backing away slowly, and discreetly trying to create a two-arm's-length distance. While one tries to bridge the gap by inching closer again, the other backs away further as their personal space is encroached upon, resulting in a hilarious cross-cultural waltz.

The British value good manners and appropriate speech, using phrases like "please," "thank you," "excuse me," and "I'm sorry" as part of their daily "vocab." Try elbowing an Englishman in the ribs accidentally on a crowded train and chances are they will end up apologizing to you. This constant need to apologize is a source of puzzlement for other cultures such as the Russians and Germans, who believe that "I'm sorry" should be reserved for times when you have legitimately hurt somebody. However, the British view these phrases as part of one's basic politeness repertoire, and frown upon anyone that doesn't use them frequently. And when you're walking along a street and step aside for someone in Britain, chances are the person you are stepping aside for may say "cheers," which is a way of showing appreciation. An appropriate response is "you're welcome" or "no problem."

If you think that you have British graciousness all worked out when you hear the words, "drop in anytime," think again. Unlike the Aussies, who will extend the invitation and expect you to drop by unannounced on your way to the store or the beach for a "cuppa," this phrase is not meant to be taken literally in Britain.

It's a better idea to telephone your British friend ahead of time and ask if it's okay to drop by before actually doing so.

In parts of England, you may be referred to by the term "duck" by a person you may not know well at all. I know, I know, you resemble nothing like the feathered, web-footed variety of the animal kingdom. Believe me when I say that this is not only normal, it is a term of endearment. You may be called *dear, dearie, love, me duck, me duckie, ma'am, madam,* or *miss.* The word "*duck*" is thought to originate from the Anglo-Saxon word "*ducis,*"which was a term of respect and denoted a leader or commander (from which came the title "Duke").

You'll find out soon enough that you can't go anywhere or do anything in Britain without someone commenting about the weather, probably because they get more rain than most places in the world. The British love their gardens, so if you're stuck for something to chat about, try gardening and/or the countryside. It will have them feeling right at home. Other safe topics of conversation include travel, music, books, sport, hobbies, food, and restaurants.

And lastly, the British never say *bathroom,* or even *restroom.* The toilet in Great Britain is called a *toilet.*

Addressing Royalty:

Worried about what title to use or how to behave when addressing the Queen or member of the Royal Family? Despite the Official Website of the British Monarchy stating, "there are no obligatory codes of behavior when meeting The Queen or a member of the Royal Family," the Australian Prime Minister set tongues wagging when she failed to curtsy to the Queen on her visit to Australia in 2011, choosing to bow her head instead. As a sign of respect, I believe it's best to stick to tradition and royal protocol, so when greeting royalty, men do a head bow and women curtsy.

The Queen (or King) is addressed as "Your Majesty," and subsequently "Ma'am" or "Sir." The other male and female members of the Royal family must be addressed as "Your Royal Highness," and subsequently "Sir" or "Ma'am." HM Queen Elizabeth II must never be referred to as "she" or "her." The Queen must always be referred to as "The Queen" or "Her Majesty."

How To Curtsy:

- First lower your head as a sign of respect.

- Place both hands on the sides of your skirt and hold it out sideways. If your skirt is narrow or you are wearing trousers, then hold your hands out to the side with your palms outward.

- Extend one foot behind the other and bend both legs at the knee. Drop down gently without leaning over to one side.

Should you wish to observe the traditional forms of Royal protocol and etiquette, ask the advice of someone well-briefed on these matters beforehand. For more information on Royal protocol, go to the Official Website of the British Monarchy on www.royal.gov.uk

The English Sense of Humor:

The most important thing in the world for the British is to be witty. To be perceived as boring is a fate worse than death. While Americans put far more importance on emotional transparency and "sincerity," tending to find British witticisms a tad pretentious, the British find open displays of emotion embarrassing and inappropriate.

The British bury their sentimentality under humor, which is what makes them the absolute masters of irony. With a unique comedic style that is dry, sarcastic, self-deprecating, and razor sharp, it is delivered with deadpan accuracy. Some famous examples of British comedy include *Mr Bean, Monty Python, Fawlty Towers, Black Adder,* and *Absolutely Fabulous.*

Conversation Taboos:

- As the English are a private and discreet people, any topic of conversation that is too personal – like religion, sex, politics, personal gossip, and asking someone their age – is considered impolite. The English are also of the belief that success and wealth should speak for themselves. The need to brag about one's success and wealth is considered crass, and a reflection of one's poor breeding and lack of education.

- The topic of the European Union (EEC) divides the population into those in favor of greater European integration, and those in favor of maintaining British sovereignty. Opinion polls show that the latter constitutes the majority view. At the risk of being subjected to a forceful debate on the subject, it's best to skip this topic altogether.

- With the British love for the Sunday roast and all things deep fried, British cuisine has been vilified through the ages as unimaginative and heavy. However, Modern British cuisine, which fully emerged in the late 1970s, uses high-quality local ingredients and combines traditional British recipes with modern innovations. So skip the ribbing on Brit cuisine already. It's old hat and inappropriate.

- With Britain never having had a post-enlightenment revolution, and its roots firmly entrenched in the monarchy, British society is still relatively obsessed with class. Avoid being critical of Britain's class distinctions. That most definitely includes being critical of the Queen and the Royal Family.

Appropriate Social Behavior:

The British concept of "fair play" extends to drinks at the pub, where you are expected to pay for your own drink, except for when someone pays for a round of drinks, wherein you're expected to pay for the next round. One can only imagine the confusion when an Englishman has drinks with a Chinese colleague, who believes that a host not only pays for all bills on the night, including entertainment, but that it is impolite to fight over the bill or split the costs.

The British love of order extends to "queues" or standing in line. Unlike the notorious-queue-jumping Russians and Israelis, the British wait patiently for their turn, no matter how long it takes. So when in Britain, refrain from skipping to the front of the queue when boarding a bus, waiting in line for a taxi, or waiting to be served at the post office, bank, or store.

British people place considerable value on punctuality, so arriving even a few minutes late for any professional appointment, or for a dinner or lunch invitation, is a big *faux pas*. Arriving early is often expected if you're attending a play, a concert, the movies, sporting events, church services, and weddings. If there's a delay, or you're unable to keep the appointment, it's best to ring your companion as early as possible prior to the event.

Gift Giving Etiquette:

Always take a gift for the host and hostess when invited for dinner. A lovely bottle of wine, bunch of flowers, or high-quality after-dinner chocolates are all acceptable gifts. A gift that is representative of your country will also be appropriate and valued, such as a beautifully handcrafted item or coffee table book.

Dining Etiquette:

In Britain, the word "dinner" in the western and northern parts of England and Wales can mean the midday meal, while "tea" refers to the early evening meal. There are no hard and fast rules, so it's a good idea to clarify what meal is being referred to when you are invited.

In general, dinners are the main meal of the day in England and would more than likely be the time when you would be invited for a meal. Sunday lunches are generally reserved for the family. It is always a good idea to advise your host of any dietary restrictions at least one week prior to the scheduled occasion, so that you can give your host enough time to make other arrangements for you.

The food in a British household may be prepared and served in one of several ways:

- Passing the serving platters from one guest to another, so that they may serve themselves.

- Buffet style, so that guests may serve themselves - usually reserved for larger numbers.

- The host plates the food individually from the kitchen and passes it to each person.

Guests are expected to wait until everyone at their table has been served before they begin to eat, with an exception made for very large groups.

Food is eaten Continental style, with a knife and fork, using the cutlery from the outside of the layout first, working your way inward to the utensils closest to the plate. Dessert is eaten with a spoon and fork. The napkin is laid across the lap, not tucked into the clothes, and definitely not used for blowing one's nose.

When eating soup, the soup bowl tilt and scoop action of the spoon should be away from you. However, when eating sweets, the action of the spoon scoop should be towards you. Just watch and observe what everyone else does if this causes you any confusion.

Whether to leave some food on your plate or to finish it all is a grey area for the English themselves. Some believe that it is polite to finish everything on your plate, a practice that stems from the food rationing in World War II, while others believe that you should leave a little behind, indicating that your host has given you more than enough food. To be on the safe side, never serve yourself more than you can manage.

After the invitation, a thank-you note or telephone call is considered polite and an appropriate way to express appreciation to your host.

High Tea Etiquette:

"There is no trouble so great or grave that cannot be much diminished by a nice cup of tea."

– BERNARD-PAUL HEROUX, 19TH CENTURY BASQUE PHILOSOPHER.

The practice of "Afternoon Tea" was traditionally taken before the evening dinner – about four o'clock – and consisted of cakes, biscuits, bread and butter, and tea. "High Tea" was taken between five and six o'clock in the afternoon, and was likely to be a replacement for the main meal. Dinner was then served as late as eight o'clock. To this day, the British reconnect with friends and family, establish new friendships, and generally cure all the ills of the world, with a soothing cup of tea.

The Palm Court Tearoom at The Ritz London has historically been one of the most sought after places to experience the tradition of "High Tea" at its best. Like The Ritz London, most tea rooms serve tea from three to five o'clock, and it consists of three particular courses served specifically in this order: savories (tiny sandwiches and appetizers), scones (served with jam and clotted cream), and pastries (cakes, cookies, and sweets).

Tea Time has its own sets of rules and etiquette, starting from the way that you hold the teacup correctly. *More useless ritual,* you may well exclaim. But holding the teacup correctly not only ensures grace, it ensures that the hot tea doesn't spill and scald your lap. So place your fingers to the front and back of the handle with your pinkie finger slightly tilted up for balance. Don't loop your fingers through the handle, or hold the body of the cup with the palm of your hand.

When stirring your tea, try not to use wide circular motions. Try using a delicate motion, without "clanging" the sides of the tea cup with your spoon, instead. Place the spoon discreetly on the right side of the saucer after stirring. Sip your tea elegantly, don't gulp it, and place the teacup back on the saucer after sipping. Avoid cupping the cup in your hand.

If you're having milk in your tea, pour it into the cup first. Avoid cream as it can mask the taste of a good tea. You can add sugar cubes to your tea with or without milk. If you prefer lemon with your tea, delicate lemon slices are generally offered with the use of a small fork. It's never a good idea to mix lemon together with milk in your tea, or you'll end up with a curdled mess in your cup. And never, ever, lick the teaspoon.

When eating scones, split the scone in half horizontally with a knife, and spread butter on the crumb side of the scone, followed by the jam and a dollop of cream if you like. And while you may be famished after all that shopping at Harrods, eat your mini-sandwiches with delicate bites, remembering to smile and chat in between.

Refrain from setting your fork back down on the table after you have used it. Set it down on the side of the plate instead. If you have to leave the table temporarily, set your napkin on your seat instead of back on the table.

Dressing Etiquette:

To say the British are avid followers of fashion is like stating that one legged ducks swim in circles. In fact, London is a fashion capital so you'd better step up your style as soon as you get off that plane. People will be friendly to you if they like the way you've put yourself together and aloof if they don't like your shirt.

Unless you're off to the gym, or are out for a jog, leave your sweats and runners back at the hotel, or risk social Siberia. If you wear jeans, make sure they're clean and up-to-the-minute in fashion, and that you accompany it with a knock-out shirt and jacket, and the right accessories. A tad confused? I've listed the best London department stores for you so that you can observe how the locals are dressing and emulate accordingly. No need to spend a fortune either.

While smart casual dress is appropriate for most visits to peoples' homes in Britain, you may want to dress more formally when attending a dinner invitation or a cultural event, such as a concert or the theatre. If you are attending High Tea, jeans are most certainly not acceptable dress for men or women. In fact, in certain establishments such at The Palm Court Tearoom at The Ritz London, you will not be admitted.

London Department Stores:

Harrods, 87–135 Brompton Road, Knightsbridge, (Harrods' food hall is a "must see"), Knightsbridge Station.

Harvey Nichols, 109–125 Knightsbridge, London, (very funky store, a must for fashionistas), Knightsbridge Station.

Selfridges, 400 Oxford Street, London, (modern store that attracts top-end shoppers), Bond St/Marble Arch Station.

Debenhams, 334–348 Oxford Street, London, (affordable ranges, an extensive lingerie section and cosmetics hall, attracts a younger clientele), Oxford Circus/Bond Street Station.

Liberty, 210–220 Regent Street, London, (definitely worth a visit, the store feels more like a luxurious home), Oxford Circus Station.

Marks & Spencer (M&S), 458 Oxford Street, London, (fine clothing range and good underwear, reasonably priced), Marble Arch Station.

Dover Street Market, 17–18 Dover Street, London (6–story Georgian fronted building in Mayfair houses designer wear and exclusive one-offs. Super funky, it's the brainchild of Rei Kawakubo of Commes des Garçons), Bond Street Station.

Ascot Races:

One hasn't truly lived in Great Britain without having experienced the races at Ascot. Ascot is a small town of Berkshire, which hosts one of the most famous thoroughbred horse race meetings in the world, the Royal Ascot. Located close to Windsor Castle, and closely associated with the British Royal Family, HM Queen Elizabeth II and other members of the British Royal Family arrive each day in a horse-drawn carriage with the Royal procession taking place at the start of each race day.

The Royal Enclosure is *the* place to be at Royal Ascot. Entry to the Royal Enclosure is by sponsorship from an existing badge-holder who has attended for four previous years. The Royal Enclosure gives you access to the best viewing areas and facilities on the course, including the gardens, where you can sit down and relax.

The dress code at The Royal Enclosure at Royal Ascot is different from the dress code on all other race days. It is formal and very strictly enforced.

Men are required to wear black or grey morning dress with a top hat. A waistcoat and tie are now compulsory in this area of the course and cravats will not be allowed. Black shoes must also be worn with morning dress.

The following are the guidelines for ladies:

- A day dress with a hat is required. As dress codes have just been tightened in Royal Ascot's Royal Enclosure, fascinators will no longer be suitable. The new dress code states that, "Hats should be worn; a headpiece which has a base of four inches (10cm) or more in diameter is acceptable as an alternative to a hat."

- Women are expected to wear skirts or dresses of 'modest length' that fall just above the knee or longer.

- Modern and stylish dress at Royal Ascot, just within the parameters of formal wear, is acceptable.

- Off the shoulder dresses, halter necks, spaghetti straps, mini-skirts, midriffs, and generally showing off too much skin, are not only unsuitable for Royal Ascot. They are banned.

- Do wear dressy closed shoes as opposed to open toes; wet hose is not a good look when the grounds are wet.

Style Tip: A word of caution regarding hats: wearing a hat that is too big, or too loud can look out of proportion with the rest of your body or outfit. So keep it simple, stylish and chic, unless you don't mind getting noticed for all the wrong reasons.

For more details on Ascot, and Royal Ascot, go to: http://www.ascot.co.uk

Safety Precautions:

Like many big cities of the world, the major cities of Great Britain have their fair share of social problems, including pickpocketing, theft (mobile phones are a favorite, often snatched by fast-moving cyclists), begging and drug abuse. Exercise the same amount of caution as you would when visiting any other city in Europe.

Loud and rowdy behavior and fights occur frequently around London, particularly on Friday and Saturday nights and after football matches. If you are harassed, it's best to ignore those concerned and walk away.

Avoid walking the streets on your own at night. Avoid befriending anyone that randomly approaches you and recommends a local bar or club. Lone visitors have been known to have been lured into a private clubs with the promise of something more than a drink. Before knowing it, a substantial "hostess fee" will appear on the victim's bill for several hundred pounds and they are not allowed to leave before paying it, sometimes with the use of force.

Street gang culture is a growing problem in a major city like London. While most groups of youngsters are not likely to present any danger to tourists, it's always best to be slightly more vigilant in certain areas, especially certain outer suburbs. Stick to the more commercial areas, where there are likely to be more people, and keep away from housing estates. Generally, outside central London, the South, and East suburban areas are considered more problematic due to crime, notably Brixton and Hackney. Hackney Wick and the surrounding areas should be avoided, becoming increasingly dangerous at night. Some parts of North-West London, such as Harlesden and northern Camden, are also known trouble spots.

Beware of scam artists, like the older gentleman asking you for directions, a man in a suit asking for emergency money for the phone, or a man with a very convincing fake gash on his arm asking for money to get to hospital.

Avoid taking illegal minicabs. If you need to take a night bus, always travel on the lower deck where it is generally safer, you are visible by the bus driver, and there are more passengers around. If you have been the victim of crime on the railways or the London

Underground, you should report the crime as soon as possible to the British Transport Police, who have an office in most major train and tube stations.

If you have been the victim of crime, you should report your crime as normal to the Metropolitan Police. For all emergencies, dial 999. http://content.met.police.uk/Home

Greece

> "I was not sure I wanted to issue orders to life; I rather liked the Greek notion of allowing Chance to take a formative hand in my affairs."
>
> **– ROBERTSON DAVIES, CANADIAN JOURNALIST AND AUTHOR.**

Historic Influences:

Greeks are extremely proud of their cultural heritage, and rightly so. One of the world's oldest civilizations, it is the cradle of Western culture as we know it. From the Cycladic, Minoan, and Mycenaean maritime civilizations, to its Classical period and military city-states of Athens and Sparta, the Greeks gave rise to many of the world's cultural emblems.

Greek ideas and culture amalgamated over the centuries with other great cultures during the rule of Alexander the Great, who marched into Asia Minor, Egypt, Persia, and what we know today as Afghanistan and India. Ruling for three dynasties, Alexander the Great's rule became known as the Macedonian Empire and Greece's Hellenistic period.

For several decades after 205BC, the powerful Romans, illustrious Byzantine Empire, and the Ottoman Turks took turns in ruling Greece, further enriching the mix. The result is the vibrant heritage that we see today.

Religion & Family Values:

Religion is integral to life in Greece, with Greek Orthodox being the national religion. Most holidays and festivals in Greece are religious in nature, with Easter being even more important than Christmas.

The family is the basis of all social structure in Greece. Grandparents are treated with dignity and respect, and the whole family shares in the nurturing, as well as disciplining, of the children. Nepotism is not only accepted, it is expected, and the family, direct and extended, are expected to help any relative in times of need. The wrongdoing of a family member can bring dishonor to the entire clan. Taking a Greek on means that you take on the entire family, so if you have any grievances, you may want to settle them as quickly and politely as possible.

Greeting & Conversation Etiquette:

The Greeks are warm, open, welcoming, and expressive in manner. When meeting them for the first time, a warm handshake with everyone in the group, men, women, and even children, along with good eye contact, is normal. Hugs, light pats on the back and shoulder, and a kiss on each cheek, even among men, is common between good friends and family members.

Greeks tend to stand very close, less than an arm's length away, when conversing with those that they know well. This may be too close for comfort for those that come from more formal cultures, like the British, Japanese or Germans. However, it is considered rude for the listener to start backing away. In addition to that, direct eye contact in conversation is expected as it indicates that the listener is engaged. You might find some comfort in the fact that the distance widens when Greeks speak with people that they don't know that well.

The Greeks are very tactile in conversation, with a fair amount of patting on the arms and shoulders between men and women, men and men, and women and women. Greeks are also demonstrative and affectionate, so public displays of affection are common.

When you want to say "yes" or "no" in Greece, say the actual words instead of just nodding your head, which is considered impolite. Remember that the nods that signify "yes" and "no" in the West are different in Greece. "Yes" is signaled by a slight nod of the head downwards, and "no"is a slight upward nod of the head. And when your Greek companion suddenly becomes quiet or withdrawn, this is definitely not a good sign. Chances are that you have said something that has offended them.

Greeks will ask you extremely personal questions about your marital status and about your family, which you may find intrusive if you happen to come from a reserved culture. They'll want to know if you're married, how many children you have, and may even ask about your income. Don't worry. This is a way of working out your family values before they welcome you into theirs.

Greeks don't take to people who are pretentious, standoffish, or who give the impression that they are above everyone else. And because Greeks are so proud, never publicly question what they say, or it will cause them great humiliation.

Remember that the American "OK" sign is considered a very rude gesture in Greece. You may want to use the "thumbs up" gesture instead to indicate 'OK'. The American gesture of "talk to the hand," extending all five fingers and palm out towards another person's face, is extremely offensive. The closer the hand to the other person's face, the more insulting.

Welcome topics of conversation would include anything to do with Greece in a positive vein: a compliment on their country, Greek history, Greek architecture, Greek cuisine and drink, the country terrain, etc.

Conversation Taboos:

- Avoid criticizing Greece or its history, the Greek way, their food, or their coffee.

- It's also best to stay away from any political topic, or discussion about Cyprus and Turkey. If they initiate the discussion, always remain diplomatic, sympathetic, and sensitive.

Appropriate Social Behavior:

Although the Greeks are not into punctuality, and will more than likely be late for any appointment, they will expect their foreign guests to be on time. Greeks are slow to trust foreigners, so the foreigner's punctuality shows respect and the first step to earning their trust.

Greeks prefer to meet face-to-face rather than telephoning as they enjoy the personal contact. If meeting over a meal or a coffee, a Greek man will always try to pay. He may give in if you are insistent, or make the arrangement ahead of time. If a foreign woman wants to invite a Greek man to lunch or dinner for the first time, it is best to invite other friends as well.

Gift Giving Etiquette:

Greeks are extremely generous, and the highest honor one can receive from them is to be invited to their home for a meal, where you will be fed and treated royally. Bring along a small gift like pastries, whiskey, a good wine, and/or a bunch of flowers.

Greeks exchange presents on name days (birth date of the saint after which they are named), as well as birthdays and Christmas. Gifts do not have to be expensive. Rather, they need to be well thought out and beautifully wrapped. Gifts are usually opened when they are received. Never give sharp objects (knives) or cheap wine as presents.

Dining Etiquette:

"It is difficult to argue with the belly, for it has no ears."

– PERICLES, STATESMAN, ORATOR AND GENERAL OF ATHENS

To be invited to a Greek's home for a meal is to be invited to the inner sanctum of their lives, their home and hearth. Consider this a great honor and dress accordingly. You may arrive 30 minutes after the stipulated time, which is considered normal arrival time for them.

The first thing that you do on arrival into their home is compliment the home. Then, offer to help the hostess with the preparation, or clearing up, of the meal. Although they may not take you up on it, it will be more than appreciated. When it is time to eat, remain standing until invited to sit down. It is a sign of respect. Ask your host where they would like you to sit.

Eating style is Continental, with the fork held in the left hand and the knife in the right. Do not begin eating until the hostess starts. As is the style in the rest of Europe, keep your elbows off the table and your hands above the table when eating.

Often, there will be communal or shared plates placed in the middle of the table, like the salads and *mezes*, a selection of small dishes served in the Mediterranean and Middle East as dinner or lunch. Go ahead and dig your fork into the communal plates, as that's what it's there for. This is more often done at family dinners and meals at the tavernas, rather than in upscale restaurants.

"Bread is a utensil in Greece", says chef Diane Kochilas, owner of Pylos restaurant in New York. The Greeks use bread for dipping into *mezes*, as well as for mopping up the delicious sauces on the plate. So go ahead and mop up the juices on your plate with your bread to your heart's content.

Don't be surprised if your fellow guests share the food from their plates with you. Likewise, it's only good manners to share some of your own food with them too. Don't be shy about accepting second helpings at a meal either, which shows your host that you are enjoying the meal. But you may want to pace yourself, as you will be offered food until you are ready to burst in every Greek meal. And leaving food on your plate means that you found something wrong with the food.

Meals are the main way that Greeks socialize, so expect a great deal of noise and vigorous discussion at the table. Quite often, especially when you're eating at a taverna, dancing will feature as part of the entertainment. Show you're a good sport and join in, even though dancing may not be your thing. Your Greek friends will love you for it. When eating out in Greece, the person who extends the invitation always pays.

With regards to toasting, the host, or man of the house, always gives the first toast, reciprocated by the honored guest later on in the meal. The most common toast is *stinygiasou*, which means "to your health." *Eis igían sas* is used at more formal functions, and means the same thing.

Finally, putting your napkin next to your plate signals that you have finished eating.

Dressing Etiquette:

The Greeks love to dress well and appreciate it when foreign guests make the same effort. Although dressing in Greece is less formal than in northern Europe, even in hot weather or casual situations, shorts and T-shirts are not acceptable. A smart casual outfit, like a pair of slacks or skirt, worn with a blouse and sandals, are appropriate for being out during the day. Dressing for dinner shows respect for the company you will be dining with. In this case a fashionable dress, or skirt and evening top, and high heels are ideal.

Safety Precautions:

Exercise caution when driving in some parts of Greece, as it can be hazardous due to poorly maintained roads and/or some aggressive drivers. This applies to most countries of the Mediterranean too. In some areas, you'll get honked at if you drive too slowly on the freeways, if you leave too much space between your car and the one in front of you,, and even if you stop at pedestrian crossings or at red lights.

When in doubt, ask one of the locals about the driving conditions in the particular city or town you are in. They may also be able to give you some tips on which no-parking zones get ticketed, and in which ones you can park without penalty. Always avoid driving on Friday and Saturday nights, by far the busiest time for traffic and pedestrians.

Like you would in any foreign country, exercise caution when walking alone, and avoid any secluded areas, especially after dark.

Pick-pocketing and bag snatching can take place in popular tourist areas and in public transport, so keep your possessions close to you at all times. As a safety precaution, never wear obviously expensive jewelry when you're out and about.

Penalties for possession, acquisition, and trafficking drugs are severe in Greece. If caught, mandatory jail term in a local prison accompanies a hefty fine.

eight

India

"India was the motherland of our race, and Sanskrit the mother of Europe's languages: she was the mother of our philosophy; mother, through the Arabs, of much of our mathematics; mother, through the Buddha, of the ideals embodied in Christianity; mother, through the village community, of self-government and democracy. Mother India is in many ways the mother of us all."

– WILL DURANT, AMERICAN HISTORIAN.

Historic Influences:

India is a huge country that consists geographically of the entire Indian Peninsula and portions of the Asian mainland. It is also one of the founding civilizations of human history. With human settlement appearing approximately 9,000 years ago, it was the only civilization able to successfully defend itself against the Mongols and Alexander the Great. But it was not until the 3rd century BC that India, united under Asoka the Great, entered into its Golden Age. This was the time that Hinduism and Buddhism were born, in addition to huge advances in mathematics, art, language, and astronomy.

India's golden period of independence came to an end by the 16th century, when countries like the United Kingdom, the Netherlands, France and Portugal began to establish themselves around the country. By 1856, the entire country became part of the British East India Company, essentially making it part of the British Empire for the next 100 years. While India attempted to throw off the shackles of colonialism in its First War of Independence in 1857, it was unsuccessful.

The citizens of India continued to push hard against British rule during the first half of the 20th century. Through Mahatma Gandhi's non-violent civil disobedience campaign, which was supported by millions, India finally gained its independence in 1947, along with Pakistan. It became a republic and drew up its own constitutions in 1950 Today, India is a member of the United Nations, is one of the few nuclear nations in the world, and has reinvented itself through economic reforms, making it one of the fastest growing economies in the world.

In a nutshell, India is a vast and diverse country of contrasts and extremes. The natural beauty of the countryside seems at odds with the grime of its cities. The unimaginable wealth of its upper classes clashes with the extreme poverty of its lower classes, and seductive Bollywood actresses fly in the face of India's socially conservative values. An ancient, mystical, and spiritual land, it continues to intoxicate intrepid travelers from all over the world.

Greeting & Conversation Etiquette:

India has more than 200 languages, with Hindi as the official language. Urdu and Punjabi are usually spoken by Sikhs and Muslims in the north, Tamil, Telugu, Kannada and Malayalam are used in the south, while Gujarati and Marathi are spoken in the west. However, with Indians often growing up learning several languages at once, English is widely used whenever a common tongue is required.

Greetings in India can get a tad complicated, and it's a big ask for tourists to remember everything. While most Indians generally greet each other formally with the *Namaste*, a slight bow with the hands pressed together in front of the face, the Sikhs greet each other with *Sat Sri Akal*, while the Muslims greet each other with *Salaam 'Alaikum*. A polite "hello" or "good morning" in English crosses all cultural barriers, so this will do just as nicely. Indians are also great readers of body language, so make sure that your demeanor and tone match your words.

When addressing someone in India, always use their title, such as Mr, Mrs, or Miss, followed by the first name. In general, Indians do not use surnames as people do in the West. For example, a woman named Amita Sharma would be called Miss Amita, or *Amita Ji* (a Punjabi term that denotes respect).

Muslims are known by their first names followed by bin (son of) or *binti* (daughter of), plus the father's first name. Sikhs use first names followed by either *Singh* (for men) or *Kaur* (for women).

Once past the formal greeting, Indians will often spend quite a lot of time on flattering approaches, small talk, and questions about country, family, and marital status. Don't be put off by this. They are merely trying to find some middle ground in order to establish a rapport and trust. If you happen to be an eloquent speaker, always maintain humility and respect in conversation, as a verbose style is off-putting to them.

Until you know the person that you are speaking with very well, be discreet about the disclosure of certain personal information that may cause your Indian host or colleague discomfort, particularly if they are fairly traditional. Although issues such as homosexuality, single motherhood, and divorce may be widely accepted in your own culture, remember that most of India is still fairly conservative.

When engaging in discussion with Indians, as with most people from the Orient, avoid expressing outright disagreement in a direct manner, like "I don't agree" or "I can't do it." This can be interpreted as being hostile and aggressive. It is best to give a more polite answer such as "I will try."

Although the showing of appreciation is valued in India, Indians do not usually use the words "thank you." This may be interpreted as rudeness and ungratefulness by foreigners, particularly after a dinner invitation. However, Indians believe that actions are performed without expectation of anything in return, and without the need for approval or validation. There are ways to show your appreciation without having to explicitly give one's thanks. For example, you can say how much you enjoyed a certain experience or a meal, or even show your appreciation in the form of a gesture instead.

Most Indians are proud of their heritage, so they will enjoy discussing their traditions and history, especially with a foreigner. Other good conversation topics include politics, cricket, and films. Skip any discussions about Indian politics if you know little about it.

The word in Hindi for "Yes" is *Han,* and "No" is *nahin.* Add *Ji* as a sign of respect to the person you are speaking to (e.g., *Han Ji* and *Nahin Ji*).

Phir milenge (pronounced *Fir Me-leng-geh*) means "See you again."

Conversation Taboos:

- It not advisable to discuss religious beliefs in India, unless it is a genuine enquiry into a certain religious practice.

- While Indians openly discuss the country's poverty, it's a different story for a foreigner to initiate the discussion, which can be seen as impolite criticism by a foreign guest of their country.

- India's relationship with its neighboring country, Pakistan, has never been a harmonious one, so it's best to avoid discussions on this topic also.

Appropriate Social Behavior:

"I like the evening in India, the one magic moment when the sun balances on the rim of the world, and the hush descends, and ten thousand civil servants drift homeward on a river of bicycles, brooding on the Lord Krishna and the cost of living."

– JAMES CAMERON, CANADIAN FILM DIRECTOR, FILM PRODUCER, SCREENWRITER, EDITOR, AND INVENTOR.

By the middle of the 21st century, India is expected to surpass China in terms of population, which equates to more business and travel opportunities between India and the West. It is important to become acquainted with Indian communication patterns and social behavior.

Non-verbal gesturing can get you into big trouble in India. Beckoning someone with the palm up and wagging one finger can be construed as an insult, while standing with your hands on your hips will be interpreted as an angry, aggressive posture. Never whistle or wink, as whistling is impolite and winking can be interpreted as either an insult or a sexual proposition.

Like the Buddhists and Muslims, feet are considered unclean in India, so never point your feet at someone. If your shoes or feet touch another person, it's important to apologize. And if the feet are considered unclean, then the head is considered the seat of the soul, so never pat or touch anyone on the head, even a child.

When you are giving something to someone in India, never toss or throw it, even if you are giving something to one of the street urchins or beggars. This is considered extremely insulting.

You will note that Indians are fastidious about washing their hands several times every day, and not just prior to any meal. Make sure that you take their lead, from a hygiene point of view as well as respect.

Gift Giving Etiquette:

Gift giving is customary in India and is seen as a sign of friendship. However, avoid giving expensive gifts unless you are very close to the person. Indians will try and reciprocate the gift and an expensive gift may only cause embarrassment for the recipient.

In India, gifts are given, and accepted, using both hands as a sign of respect. Gifts are also never opened at the time that they're received, so don't insist that your host opens the gift that you have given them. If you are the recipient of a gift, put it aside until the giver leaves.

Unless your Hindu host is very traditional, the giving of leather gifts, like a handbag or belt, is no longer considered offensive. However, use your common sense. Handbags or belts are fairly personal items, and may not be the most appropriate present to give your host. Try bringing them something that is typical, and of a high quality, from your country. If your host has children, bringing a gift for each child, such as a toy or a book, will always be appreciated.

Although some Hindus may drink alcohol, especially if Westernized, it is best not to offer a gift of alcohol unless you have verified from the recipient of the gift that alcohol would be an acceptable gift. If it is, you could give them a bottle of scotch whisky or fine wine. Exercise some caution with this, as many

Indians may drink when traveling abroad, but will not imbibe when in their home country.

If you are invited to an Indian's home for dinner, a box of chocolates or flowers are appropriate gifts, while a box of sweets is customary if you are visiting an Indian during a festival.

Regarding flowers, always check with a local florist what is the appropriate flower to give for specific occasions. Marigolds, especially in a garland, are inappropriate as they are used for prayer ceremonies, temple decor, and to honor the deceased. White is also the color of grieving. A bouquet of roses is a safe choice, as are lilies and gerberas.

Dining Etiquette:

In India, the dining experience is enhanced with the use of fingers as opposed to cutlery. Many times, a spoon is used in conjunction with fingers, so that the delicious soups and liquids from the food can be scooped up and savored. This may feel strange to the Westerner at first, but let your inhibitions go, as the experience will truly be a feast of the senses. The most important thing is to sample the different dishes separately so as to appreciate their individual flavors. Just don't forget to wash your hands before you start eating.

Guests of honor are always seated first at the table. If you are dining with Muslims, eating is done with the right hand as the left hand is considered unclean. Remember never to pass or receive anything with your left hand, and never lick your fingers, or sample the food from someone else's plate.

An Indian meal consists mainly of the following: Indian bread (*chapati, roti,* or *naan*), side dishes (salad, *papad,* and pickles), main dishes of vegetables and/or meat, Dal (a lentil dish), and rice. Hindus do not eat beef and Muslims do not eat pork.

It is best to eat smaller portions of food at the beginning of your meal as you will be offered more food later on, and it's only good manners for you to accept. Not finishing everything on your plate will not cause offense either, although you may want to wait until everyone has finished before getting up to wash your hands.

If you happen to let a little belch escape your lips, don't panic. Burping in India after a meal isn't considered rude, as it would be in France or Great Britain. It is actually seen as a sign of contentment.

Unlike the Chinese and Japanese, the Indians are not big on drinking alcohol. Alcohol is culturally not accepted in most parts of India, and many Indians do not even drink at home.

At the end of a meal, refrain from saying "thank you" to your hosts. As previously mentioned, "thank you" denotes a form of payment on the part of the guest, and the act of giving in India is done without expectation of return. What you can do is to mention how much you enjoyed a particular part of the meal, or compliment the host on the lovely experience. You will hit the mark with your compliments.

Dressing Etiquette:

How a woman dresses in India will directly affect the way that she is treated. For this reason, it's important to do your own home-work on the accepted dress code. Your Indian friends may be too polite to tell you that you are inappropriately dressed, even when they are asked directly.

Clothing for women should be loose, never tight, and it's consid-ered unacceptable to show your legs, upper arms, chest, or back. The ONLY time it's acceptable for your midriff to be exposed is when wearing a sari, but not otherwise. I know, I know, this from the country that brings sultry and seductive Bollywood actresses to the world. I did say that India was a country of contrasts, didn't I? But believe me, this dressing tip is well worth following; ignoring it may bring you plenty of unwanted attention from local men. Loose clothing is more comfortable in the tropical heat in any case.

Okay, it's time to get really specific here about dress etiquette in India. Always wear a bra underneath your clothing, even though you may not be exactly buxom. Wearing sleeveless shirts, halter neck or tank tops, shorts, short skirts, or any tight clothing, are real no-nos in India. They will only invite stares, lewd comments, and cat calls.

Longer skirts – ankle or calf length – in cool fabrics with loose fitting long-sleeved tops are considered appropriate dress, so long as the fabric is not transparent. Skirts are easier than pants in India if you have to use the traditional Indian toilets, where one needs to squat (sorry to get so graphic).

A *Salwar Kameez,* also referred to as a Punjabi suit, is an attractive dress-and-pant outfit worn by Sikhs and some Hindu women in India. I highly recommend that you get yourself a couple to wear on your Indian trip as they are beautiful as well as comfortable and modest. The shawl can be draped around the chest and shoulders for modesty purposes, or used as a headdress when visiting temples or mosques. You can buy them almost anywhere in India, but it's best to buy some cloth at a store and have a tailor make it to your specifications. I strongly recommend that you choose darker colors as opposed to pastels, as you will get unavoidably covered with dust.

A *sari* is a dress worn primarily by Hindu women consisting of a blouse, sari petticoat, and several yards of light material draped around the body. When wearing a *sari,* do not wear the *sari* petticoat and blouse on their own without the yards of material that drapes around the body. This is a mistake many foreign women make, and it is the equivalent of walking down the street in your underwear.

If you decide to wear jeans and a shirt, then make sure that the shirt has short sleeves – never sleeveless or capped – and that the shirt is left untucked and covers your crotch area and your back side. Similarly, when wearing a pantsuit, make sure that the pants are loose and not tight, and your blouse covers the crotch area and back side.

Always wear sunglasses when you're out in public. Not only are they good for eye protection from the harsh sun, dust, and smog, they also stop you from meeting men's eyes, an action that can be interpreted as flirtation in the more conservative parts of India. It's also a good idea to carry a large scarf or pashmina with you as they are good for draping over your neck, shoulders and head for modesty when visiting a temple, or to maintain some level of personal space when you're in a crowd or riding in public transport.

Sandals or slip-on shoes are the footwear of choice when visiting a local person's home or temples, as it is customary to take one's shoes off when entering these places. Although the cow is considered sacred to devout Hindus, the use of leather goods in India (shoes, sandals, and handbags) is no longer such a taboo.

When wearing a swimsuit at the beach or hotel pool, do wear a one-piece rather than a bikini, and bring a modest cover-up that you can slip on when you are out of the water.

Safety Precautions:

The first thing you will notice in India is the number of street urchins and beggars that will approach your car when you are stopped at traffic lights. Avoid giving them money, as more than likely the money will go towards an organized scam. Instead, carry food in tidy packages, like small packets of glucose biscuits, bananas, and even lifesavers. This way, the children can at least get some nourishment from you as they won't be benefiting from any money that you give them.

If you happen to be a blonde, red head, or have a fair complexion, be prepared to be stared at. Indian men love to stare, particularly in the more conservative areas. They mean no harm. Just behave and dress modestly, avoid direct eye contact with the local men in public, and go about your business as usual.

When you are being approached or harassed by young males, the phrase to use is *Nahin Ji*, which means "No thanks" in the most respectful way possible. Even saying it in English is acceptable. The key is to keep your voice intonation respectful, while not making eye contact and continuing to move forward. Do not use the phrase *chale jao* (pronounced *chelo*), which I have seen recommended on other resources over the net. This means "go away" in the rudest possible way. This will only antagonize and encourage them to become more vocal.

Some women find it helpful to wear fake wedding rings to keep men at bay, as in India, being connected to a man commands respect for a woman.

nine

Israel

"Israel is the very embodiment of Jewish continuity: It is the only nation on earth that inhabits the same land, bears the same name, speaks the same language, and worships the same God that it did 3,000 years ago. You dig the soil and you find pottery from Davidic times, coins from Bar Kokhba, and 2,000-year-old scrolls written in a script remarkably like the one that today advertises ice cream at the corner candy store."

– CHARLES KRAUTHAMMER, AMERICAN PULITZER PRIZE-WINNING SYNDICATED COLUMNIST, POLITICAL COMMENTATOR, AND PHYSICIAN.

Historic Influences:

The people of Israel can trace their origins to Abraham (ca. 1800 BC), who established the belief that there is only one god. Abraham, his son Yitshak (Isaac), and grandson Jacob (Israel), are referred to as the patriarchs of the Israelites. The descendants of Abraham came together as a nation after their Exodus from Egypt in 1300 BC, under the leadership of Moses.

While in exile in the Sinai desert, Moses transmitted to his people the foundations of the Jewish religion, the Torah and the Ten Commandments. After 40 years in the desert, Moses led his people to the Land of Israel, which the *Bible* refers to as the "Promised Land."

After 3,300 years, the people of Israel still share the same language and culture shaped by their Jewish heritage and religion in the days of Abraham. Israel is the only country in the world where the majority of its citizens are Jewish. The *Torah*, which translates as "law," is more than just a book of rules. It is the framework for Hebrew, the Jewish religion, Jewish thought, and its society.

Israelis are often likened to the *sabra* – a term that refers to native born Israelis but literally means a cactus fruit – thorny and tough on the outside, but soft on the inside. Little wonder, when you have a state the size of New Jersey (at 7,850 square miles or 12,633 kilometers) that is dominated by the Negev Desert (4,633 square miles or 7,456km), and bordered by the Mediterranean Sea and the predominantly Muslim nations of Egypt, Jordan, Lebanon, and Syria.

Structure of Israeli Society:

Significant segments of Israeli society are religious. But within that whole, you have the Secular Jewish community, which has a predominantly Western value system, and the Orthodox Jewish community, which differs culturally from the more secular members of society.

The easiest way to tell the difference between secular Jews and the Orthodox Jews is by the way that they dress. Secular Jewish women dress no differently to women in the West, while the men, also in standard Western dress, wear a crocheted *kippa* or *yarmulke*, the slightly-rounded skullcap traditionally worn at all times by observant Jewish men.

The Orthodox Jews dress in a manner that reflects life as stipulated in the Torah, and according to traditions accumulated over several thousand years (e.g., the Torah makes no stipulation to wear black, but this is a tradition from the culture of European Jewry, dating back hundreds of years). Males wear black clothes and allow their beards to grow. Some pious (Chassidic) Jews wear ear locks, which is an interpretation of the law to mean that the "corners of the face" may not be shaved. A prayer belt, called a *gartel* in German or Yiddish, is worn to indicate the separation between what is divine (the head) from the more earthly pursuits (the bottom half of the body). It is not appropriate for Orthodox Jewish males to wear short pants.

For Orthodox Jewish women, clothing must reach up to the collar bone in the front, and to just below the nape of the neck in the back. Sleeves must always cover the elbows. Skirts (not pants) must extend below the knees, with legs covered in stockings. More subtle colors are preferred to anything that is overly bright. Clothing that is too tight or in any way revealing is a real no-no. Jewish law also requires married women to cover their hair.

Greeting & Conversation Etiquette:

You'll find the Israelis are far more forward in initiating conversations with strangers than in other Western countries. They are not big on small talk, although they will openly ask extremely personal questions, like your marital status and age. Visitors to Israel frequently find such a raw and open way of relating quite confronting. No offense is meant, so take it in the spirit that it is given.

Israelis are big on discussion and debate. Their manner of communication is direct, upfront, and honest to the point of bluntness – some tourists would even argue that they are rude. They are passionate, even forceful, when engaged in a discussion that they can sink their teeth into, complete with all the Mediterranean mannerisms of arm waving and back slapping. Hugs and kisses are fairly common.

Flexible and non-structured in their conversation topics, Israelis are naturally curious. They enjoy connecting with foreign guests on a variety of subjects such as the guest's home country, lifestyle, and his or her family. They are also fond of talking about politics. Just ask any taxi driver, who'll gladly volunteer their opinion on how the country should be run. However, when broaching the topic of politics with an Israeli, make sure that it is done with an open mind, a genuine curiosity and, most of all, respect.

Other topics that Israelis love to talk about are traveling, cuisine, the arts, technology, and sports. As you would in the West, gauge your conversation according to the degree of familiarity with the person that you are speaking with, or the degree of conservatism.

Learning the basic greeting is always a sign of respect in whichever country you are in. Here are a few phrases that will get you by in Israel:

Toda – Thank you

Ken – Yes

Lo – No

Bevakasha – Please

Shalom – Hello & Goodbye, and also means "peace."

L'chayim – The traditional toast which means "to life."

Conversation Taboos:

By and large, Israelis love to talk about politics, particularly with foreigners. However, unless your opinion is non-critical and your approach is sensitive, avoid bringing up the hot topics of politics and religion. Any discussion that is not well researched or compassionate will be met with some hostility.

Appropriate Social Behavior:

"Asked to make a list of the men who have most dominated the thinking of the modern world, many educated people would name Freud, Einstein, Marx and Darwin. Of these four, only Darwin was not Jewish. In a world where Jews are only a tiny percentage of the population, what is the secret of the disproportionate importance the Jews have had in the history of Western culture?"

– ERNEST VAN DEN HAAG, DUTCH-AMERICAN SOCIOLOGIST, SOCIAL CRITIC.

Israelis tend to rush about at a hectic pace, have a general dislike for waiting, and are notoriously impatient when they have to line up for anything. In fact, they don't usually line up for anything at all, which can drive some foreigners to distraction. It's a good idea for visitors, however, not to take this behavior to heart.

Hand gestures and language that are considered offensive in the West are considered just as offensive in Israel.

Within secular Jewish society and mostly in the Orthodox, women in Israel enjoy the same status as men. Men and women are seated at the same table and speak openly and animatedly at meal times, even in the more traditional households. The only place that men and women are separated is in synagogues, and during religious celebrations like weddings.

Refrain from taking photographs of any Israeli, Secular or Jewish, without their express permission. Although there is no religious issue associated with it, asking for permission is just a sign of respect. No one from any country likes to feel like an animal in a zoo.

The Israelis love to bargain, which is consistent with the culture of the desert. So *do* bargain enthusiastically when visiting Israeli markets, as they would expect nothing less.

Appropriate Behavior/Secular Jews:

Among Israel's secular majority, eye contact, courteous greetings, an occasional sensitive touch, handshakes, smiles, courteous compliments, and subtle, non-obtrusive gestures between men and women are all acceptable and common forms of greeting and public behavior. This behavior would be no different to what is practiced in any Western country or society.

Appropriate Behavior/Orthodox Jews:

When visiting Orthodox Religious Communities, the social practices are similar to those Muslim customs and practices, in that dress and behavior must be modest at all times (refer to section on Dressing Etiquette for more detail).

Negiah is a Hebrew word that literally means "touch." Traditional Judaism stipulates that members of the opposite sex who are not close relatives, or married, must not touch. Although some people may feel that this is extreme, traditional Judaism recognizes touch as being a powerful force, and is thus only acceptable and appropriate between two people who love each other. Touching can also create an illusory intimacy between the wrong people, thus creating problems. The term *shomer negiah* literally means saving touch for the right person. Based on this belief, visitors must refrain from greeting, touching, or extending a handshake to devout Jewish men and women. Instead, they should just greet verbally. However, touch between man and man, woman and woman, and between relatives and children are completely acceptable and normal.

Gift Giving Etiquette:

Gift giving is not lavish in Israel. When invited for a meal at someone's home, bringing a bottle of wine is considered sufficient. However, both the wine and food need to be *kosher* in Israel, even in a social setting. The word *kosher* refers to what is "fit" or "proper" under Jewish Rabbinical law. The foods that meet these stringent regulations are called *kosher* foods and have *kosher* labels.

To make sure that your wine is *kosher,* only buy wine-based drinks that are prepared and bottled by Jews. However, it is not necessary for other types of alcoholic beverages to be *kosher,* so a fine bottle of liquor makes a great gift for a Jewish friend, client, or associate if they drink. To guarantee you'll be giving an acceptable gift, any gift of food, wine, or fruit should be purchased at a store in Israel, all of which are *kosher* (with the exception of Arab owned and run stores in Arab cities and villages).

Jews are not allowed to eat pork and shellfish. Therefore, leather items made from pig skin cannot be given as a gift, nor any food from these two groups. Also avoid giving gifts made with shell/ Mother of Pearl.

If you have been invited to a wedding or *bar mitzvah,* money is usually given in the form of cash or a check, which can be placed by guests in a safe at the function hall. The amounts given can differ from family to family, so *do* ask for guidance on the appropriate amount.

Dining Etiquette:

"The only thing chicken about Israel is their soup."

– BOB HOPE, AMERICAN COMEDIAN.

Jewish men and women always dine together at the table. The only times that women and men might dine separately would be during religious celebrations, like a wedding. Western utensils are used throughout Israel and dining is done the Continental way, with a knife and fork. Similar to the West, the host sits at the head of the table, with the honored guest seated next to the host.

Unless you are told otherwise, assume that your hosts observe *kashrut,* or the eating of *kosher* food. This means that certain food items are forbidden: pork and shellfish, and the mixing of milk and meat products. After eating a meat dish, refrain from asking for butter for your bread, or milk for your coffee.

If you are inviting your Jewish friends or associates to a restaurant for a meal, avoid scheduling the lunch or dinner on *Shabbat* or any other religious festival, particularly if they are religious.

Rules of Shabbat:

Shabbat is the Jewish Holy Day. It begins on Friday evening and ends on Saturday evening. All public offices and most private businesses, including restaurants, shops, and public transport, close down. It is also considered discourteous to smoke on *Shabbat.*

Always check whether certain museums and shops close during *Shabbat,* as the schedules may vary. Regarding restaurants, many will remain open, unless they are strictly *kosher.* If you're unsure about a particular restaurant, check with the Concierge at your hotel, or with your host.

Dressing Etiquette:

Except for neighborhoods where Orthodox Jewish communities reside, Tel Aviv is a very liberal city. It is, therefore, acceptable to wear anything here that you would wear in any Mediterranean resort or town, including shorts and T-shirts. Coat and ties for men are almost unheard of. Even clerks in government offices and banks dress down, often in jeans. It is rare to see anyone in uniform in Israel, save for the soldiers.

Because of the intense heat, it's best to pack cotton or linen clothes that will keep you cooler and more comfortable. Don't forget a wide-brimmed hat, as baseball caps won't cover the back of your neck.

Dressing is not as liberal in the Orthodox Jewish communities. Living in separate neighborhoods to the secular majority, traditional Jews have their own rules and customs that foreign guests are expected to adhere to when in their neighborhoods, like *Mea Sherim* in Jerusalem. In such areas the exposure of any flesh, apart from the hands and face, is considered unacceptable, as are trousers and jeans. Examples of acceptable dress are long skirts and blouses with sleeves below the elbows.

Parts of Jerusalem are very conservative, particularly around the holy sites. In these zones, it is best to conform to "modest" dress standards. Trousers and jeans worn with long tops that cover the crotch and backside area, or longer length skirts, are acceptable, so long as the chest, arms, and shoulder areas are well covered. Otherwise, you will risk unwanted attention.

When visiting mosques, synagogues, or churches, remember not to wear anything short, tight, or in any way revealing. Carry with you a simple cotton scarf in your bag that can be thrown over your head. You may be refused entry if you are not modestly dressed.

Safety Precautions:

It is generally safe to travel to Israel. In fact, three million tourists come and go from Israel every year. However, the Israelis takes their security responsibility very seriously, so always adhere to regulations and respect the local authority. It's also best to check for security updates on your country's government website prior to traveling to Israel.

Never photograph any military or police personnel, or military installations, as local officials will more than likely consider such behavior suspicious will act accordingly.

Refrain from traveling to areas around the Gaza Strip in southern Israel, due to the high risk of violence, air strikes, mortar and rocket fire. Unless there is a specific reason for you to go to the Gaza Strip (e.g., an official posting), this area is off-limits to foreign visitors and tourists.

The West Bank is known as the territory of Samaria and Judea, which has great historical and religious significance for Jews, Muslims, and Christians alike. Although Bethlehem is part of the West Bank, Jerusalem is right on the border, but not actually in it. Most of the West Bank has been under Israeli military occupation since 1967.

If you have a great desire to visit the sacred sites in the West Bank, then your safest bet would be to travel with an organized tour group. Avoid going on your own. Apart from these specific areas, reconsider your need to travel to the West Bank. If in doubt, it's always best to check with Israeli authorities first before planning your trip. When visiting these areas, Muslim customs must be respected.

ten

Italy

> "What is the fatal charm of Italy? What do we find there that can be found nowhere else? I believe it is a certain permission to be human, which other places, other countries, lost long ago."
>
> **– ERICA JONG, AMERICAN AUTHOR, POET, ESSAYIST.**

Historic Influences:

The Italians have a long and proud history, with archeological findings showing that parts of Italy were inhabited as far back as 200,000 years ago. It was the Etruscans, however, that rose to heights of prosperity and power around 750BC; their territory spreading from present-day Tuscany north almost to Venice and south into the Campania region, only for their culture to mysteriously disappear around 500BC. Around the 8th century BC, the ancient Greeks colonized the southernmost points of mainland Italy and Sicily. The Romans later referred to this area as *Magna Graecia,* or greater Greece.

But when one refers to Italian history, one automatically conjures up visions of the magnificent Roman Empire, or *Imperium Romanum* as it was known in Latin. With its beginnings in 27 BC and lasting for approximately 422 years, the Western Roman

Empire was characterized by an autocratic government, spreading its tentacles across Europe and the Mediterranean, forming one of the greatest empires the world has ever known.

Like all sovereignties, the Roman empire had its day and eventually went into decline, and Italy once again turned itself back into a patchwork of city-states. Haphazard leadership led to a plethora of in-fighting between neighboring cities. Some city-states chose to keep the power in the hands of a group of people representing the city, while others opted to give the power to one man or a family dynasty, in the hope of maintaining some semblance of order. Known as the Dark or Middle Ages, a period of transition for Italy, some city-states like Venice and Genoa enjoyed great affluence due to their ports becoming vital to world trade routes.

The period that followed the Dark Ages between the 14th and 17th centuries became known as the Renaissance, or "rebirth.". Originating in Florence, we recognize this period by the brilliant artists that flourished at the time, such as Michelangelo, Botticelli, Titian, and Leonardo da Vinci. During the Renaissance, scholars, artists, thinkers, and philosophers gained inspiration by going back to the classics. Money and art went hand-in-hand as artists and thinkers depended on wealthy patrons, like the Medicis, in order to survive and continue creating.

From the 16th to the late 19th centuries, Italy was fought over and ruled by a succession of foreign powers, including the French and Spanish Bourbon Dynasties. It was not until 1861 that the Kingdom of Italy was formed under Victor Emmanuel II of the House of Savoy, with the support of Count Cavour and Giuseppe Garibaldi. Still, it would take many more years before the entire peninsula would be united under the Kingdom of Italy. By the 1920s the Fascist dictatorship of Benito Mussolini defeated the King and Italy eventually dissolved the monarchy. In 1946 the

Italian Republic was formed and two years later adopted its new constitution.

The Vatican:

The Vatican City State is a landlocked sovereign city-state of 44 hectares (110 acres) that sits within a walled enclave in the city of Rome. The Vatican, or The Holy See as it is referred to by Catholics, is the home of the Pope, who is the world head of the Catholic church. With a population of just 900, made up of churchmen, volunteers for the Papal court and their families, it is considered a separate state. It has its own currency, flag, stamps, and security. One can only become a citizen of the Vatican on the grounds of appointment to work in a certain capacity in the service of the Holy See.

The Vatican stance in world affairs remains officially neutral, mediating disputes only when asked to do so. There is little crime in the Vatican City. The Swiss Guard, dressed in medieval uniform, protect the city and the Pope.

Established in the 15th century, the Swiss Guard were known for their discipline and unwavering loyalty to their employers. They originally served as body guards and palace guards at the European courts. The Papal Swiss Guard in the Vatican was founded in 1506 and is the only Swiss Guard that exists today.

The ethos of the Vatican is male dominated, with men holding the vast majority of the positions in office. The married workers in the Vatican live with their families outside the Vatican walls and commute in everyday.

The required etiquette of the Vatican is the same as if you were visiting any sacred place in the world. Modest and appropriate dress for men and women is required. Shoulders and arms must be covered, and the wearing of shorts, and skirts above the knee, is highly inappropriate. Deference, respect, and silence is expected in the chapels and sacred areas, and one should speak only when addressed by the clerics and senior officials.

The Italian Concept Of Bella Figura

From modesty and humility at the Vatican to the Italian concept of *Bella Figura*. What does *Bella Figura* mean?

Bella Figura is one of the mainstays of Italian social etiquette, and it is not class specific. Referring to the way one looks and projects oneself, *Bella Figura* is all about making a good impression. It starts from a sharp and well-groomed outward appearance and goes all the way to conducting oneself with a degree of eloquence, knowledge, sophistication, and quiet confidence. With a history littered with political unrest and social upheavals, multiple political parties,, and a government riddled with accusations of corruption, so long as the modern day Italian maintains their *Bella Figura*, they can take anything in their stride.

Here are some steps that will help you maintain a *Bella Figura*. As you will see, it's not just about looking good:

- Dress simply but elegantly. Less is always more, so long as it is of good quality. Your clothing must exude a quiet glamor, a whisper rather than a shout.

- Strike a balance with the choice of colors in your wardrobe and combine it all with the right shoes and accessories. Never over-accessorize.

- Don't forget your dark glasses. Squinting does not help to maintain a *Bella Figura*.

- Conduct yourself with dignity and discretion at all times. Be charming, polite and know the rules of etiquette demanded by Italian society.

Greeting & Conversation Etiquette:

Italians are open, bold, lively and passionate communicators. Indeed, they are said to employ the most body language of all European nations. Although you are expected to engage yourself in a similar manner in more casual situations, a more subdued and controlled bearing would be expected in more formal occasions. Always be prepared to adapt yourself to the occasion.

With your chances of being judged on first impressions in Italy, first introductions and meetings are crucial. When greeting an Italian, make sure that you retain direct eye contact while shaking hands or engaging in conversation. Your handshake should be firm and enthusiastic, and make sure that you shake hands with everyone present: men, women, and children. Women must always extend their hand first. Friends may hug, slap each other on the shoulder for men, or kiss on each cheek for women.

When introducing a group of people, always introduce the most senior members of the group first out of respect, followed by the women, and then any other members present. The more formal address is *Signore* for men, and *Signora* for women, followed by the family name. You may address someone by their first name if this is how they have introduced themselves to you. Otherwise, stick to their gender title and surname until given permission as a sign of respect.

The word *Ciao* is a common greeting and way of saying goodbye throughout Italy. However, if you pay closer attention, you'll see that it's used among people who know each other well, or are in the same peer group. Among strangers, or when addressing an elder, always use more formal greetings, like *buon giorno* (good morning), *buon pomeriggio* (good afternoon), or *buona sera* (good evening), followed by their name.

Italians find it just as easy to chat with new acquaintances as with close friends, with people jumping into the conversation with new thoughts or ideas, and speaking all at once. You too will be expected to "jump in," so don't wait to be asked. In fact, Italians often feel uncomfortable with silence.

Welcome topics of conversation in Italy include Italian architecture, Italian arts and film, soccer or football, Italian food and wine, the opera, culture, history, and current events in your own country.

Conversation Taboos:

- Steer clear from discussing Italian politics, especially bringing up accusations of corruption. This is a conversational minefield - as is that other Italian organization, the Mafia.

- The Catholic Church has a very strong presence in Italy, so religion is a frequent topic of conversation for many Italians. However, criticizing the Vatican, its policies, and what it stands for, are no-go zones.

- Steer clear of topics on World War II and Italy's involvement, discussions of negative Italian stereotypes, negative aspects of Italian culture and any of its inefficiencies.

- Although Italians are hardly prudish and are well-versed on all aspects of *amoré,* avoid telling off color jokes or discussing any topic of a sexual nature. It is considered in very bad taste and your comments will be met with an embarrassed silence.

- Avoid any discussions on the differences between the northern Italians and those from the south. There is a strict order on who can say what about whom, so it's best not to step into this arena at all.

- Although discussion or inquiry about someone's profession, income, or economic situation, may be acceptable in the United States, it will be considered rude and overly personal in Italy, particularly when meeting someone for the first time.

The Family:

In Italy, the family unit, or *la famiglia*, is the glue that holds society together, with the mother reigning supreme as the dominant figure in the household. All Italians consider the mother's role to be sacred.

If home, hearth and mother are the nucleus of every Italian's life, then there is no greater pleasure for an Italian than sharing a good meal with the whole family, either in the family home or a restaurant. Great preparations go into these sit-down meals, with a meticulously set table, an assortment of mouthwatering delicacies, and conversation flowing with abandon.

The Italians love their families and revere the elderly. Always stand when an older person enters the room, greet them first before anyone else in a social or official circle, and defer to them. Similarly, children in Italy are adored. When greeting a group, always include the children. When in a social setting, always give attention to, or bring a small gift for the children.

Appropriate Social Behavior:

The Italians are a very proud people who revel in their culture and take pride in their creative achievements. They take their personal relationships seriously, with loyalty being highly valued. Openly curious and understanding of most things, they will excuse inefficiencies, absolve lateness, and forgive sincere mistakes with self-deprecating humor. However, they will not tolerate arrogance, rudeness, and bad manners.

Preferring to deal with those that they know and trust, personal relationships are of utmost importance to the Italians. Take the time and patience to foster this trust by being thoughtful, (e.g., inquiring about their family or children), and attention to detail, (e.g., bringing little gifts when visiting their home).

Although the Italian attitude towards time and punctuality can be fairly relaxed, they expect foreigners to be on time for official appointments. Call with a valid explanation if you expect to be delayed for your appointment, or your lateness will be viewed as sloppy.

The Italians believe that work should never be a burden or be taken too seriously. With this national mindset, it comes as no surprise that the Italian legal system and bureaucracy are notoriously slow, so do not expect things to happen quickly in Italy. Instead, do what the Italians do; maintain your cool and *Bella Figura*. And never call an Italian about a business or official matter at home unless it is an absolute emergency.

The Italians are generally not inhibited when interacting with the opposite sex and are born flirts. In fact, they wrote the bible on flirting. They have the unfair advantage of being blessed with ravishingly good looks, with style oozing from every pore, and can hold a gaze longer than any other culture in the history of man. If you're a single woman traveling throughout Italy, you'll either have one helluva vacation, or have your heart broken repeatedly, whichever way you want to play it.

Gift Giving Etiquette:

Italians are extremely generous, especially with their gifts. They also appreciate beauty and high quality. With this in mind, never give an Italian a present that is cheap or even practical as you will end up embarrassing yourself as well as your host. Some gift ideas include high quality liquor or wine, or an exquisite coffee table book or hand-crafted item from your country. Make sure that your gift is beautifully wrapped, although never with a gold ribbon, which symbolizes mourning. Gifts are almost always opened by the receiver when they receive it.

Dinner or lunch invitations are a great time to bring your hosts some chocolates, pastries, and/or a lovely bunch of flowers. When giving flowers, always give an uneven number. It's also worth remembering that chrysanthemums are a symbol of death, and red roses represent love and passion.

Dining Etiquette:

"Chi be vive, ben muore." (Translates to: "A good life makes a good death.")

– ITALIAN SAYING

Eating and dining is an integral part of Italian everyday life, with children being taught proper table manners from an early age. They not only savor, but take great pride, in their regional delicacies and cuisines.

The first rule when dining in an Italian home is to arrive 15 to 30 minutes after the stipulated time. Secondly, never arrive empty-handed. As discussed in the Gift Giving section, always bring a small gift for your host or a bunch of flowers. Feel free to ask for a little tour when you arrive as Italians are proud of their homes.

The intense regionality of Italy, which originated in its long history of city-states, shows its face in Italy's cuisine, language and art. Italian food differs greatly from region to region. In the north, flat and ribbon-shaped pastas are served with creamier sauces, while in the south, tomato-based sauces are more popular.

There are certain unspoken rules in Italy regarding food combinations and what to eat when. Meals usually begin with a pasta dish, followed by either meat or fish. A lighter meal may also consist of *antipasto*, meaning "appetizers," that include olives, cold meats such as prosciutto and salami, and some vegetables such as artichoke hearts. Soups sometimes take the spot of pasta as a first meal, while pizza is eaten as a snack or light meal.

Cappuccino is considered a breakfast drink only and is never drunk after lunch or dinner, whereas *caffe*, which means an espresso, can be ordered anytime of the day. Italians also drink water and wine at mealtimes, and soft drinks and beer with pizza.

The style of eating in Italy is Continental, with the fork held in the left hand and the knife in the right. It is considered polite to keep both hands on the table, never on your lap. Elbows must be off the table.

Bread plates are not normally used in casual situations. Instead, Italians like to break the bread and place it next to their plate on the table.

Wine is commonly served with all meals except breakfast. Your glass will always be topped up if it appears half full, or close to empty, at any stage. If you don't wish to drink anymore, just leave your glass relatively full. Avoid refusing a top up outrightly. Never help yourself to wine if you are a guest, particularly if you are a woman. It is considered unfeminine.

When shown to your place at a dinner table, wait for your host to be seated before seating yourself. Never begin eating, or leave the table at the end of the meal, before your host does.

The correct way to eat pasta is by using your fork to roll the pasta on the sides of your pasta plate. Never roll it on the spoon.

Avoid using your hands when picking up cheese or fruit, as it's considered unsanitary. Use a knife to pick the cheese up before transferring it to your biscuit. Similarly, fruit is always eaten with a fruit fork and knife, except for grapes and cherries.

When finished eating, place knife and fork side-by-side on the plate, with the fork on the left and the knife on the right, with the knife blade facing the fork

Drinking Etiquette:

Although known for *La Buona Vita* ("the good life") and its culture of wining and dining, the culture of drinking alcohol in Italy vastly differs to that of other Anglo-Saxon cultures. For starters, drinking without eating is not common in Italy. Neither are cocktails or "happy hour." Hard drinking, or even getting tipsy, is considered ill-mannered and an affront to the concept of *Bella Figura*. Women drink very little in Italy and do not propose toasts in formal occasions.

The Concept Of Fare i Complimenti:

If you want to blend in well with the locals as you enjoy an overabundance of good food and wine, you'll need to know about *fare i complimenti*. Practiced by all Italians with good manners, it literally translates to "making compliments." It roughly means to make good manners. More a social theatrical display than subtle code, it can be better explained by giving examples. If an acquaintance invites you for dinner at his or her place, you should not automatically respond with, "Yes, I'd love to!" This would be far too obvious. Rather, you should respectfully say, "That may be too much bother for you." This gives the other person a chance to insist with their invitation, and it is at this point that you should accept.

Another example of *fare i complimenti* is when having dinner, if your host asks you whether you want some more pasta or wine, you are supposed to respectfully decline. This allows the host to repeat his or her offer, after which you can decide whether you want to accept it or not. The further south in Italy you go, the more rooted this tradition is.

The only example where *fare i complimenti* is never used is when one is invited to drink an espresso. One never refuses a cup of espresso in Italy, or you risk being called unsociable. However, if you happen to not like coffee, you might want to decline by saying that you've drunk too much already.

Dressing Etiquette:

With Rome and Milan being two of the major fashion capitals of the world, saying that the Italians know about style is like stating that the Pope is Catholic. Even people in the small villages spend money on dressing well. But the Italian elegance is about being refined and sophisticated, never ostentatious or showy. Their clothes are faultlessly cut, meticulously made and worn with a quiet confidence. Old, torn, or unkempt clothes or appearances are not appreciated in Italy, and rest assured that the way you dress will impact on how you will be perceived by the Italians.

Italians dress for the seasons and tend to dress warmer than Americans. With the Florentines dressing more conservatively than the Romans, you can't go wrong with building your wardrobe around black, brown, and ivory, and adding some subtle color with beautiful silk scarves or a cashmere wrap. Less is more, quality over quantity. Pay attention to your shoes and bags as their quality will make or break the impression that you make. Forget about running around Italy in "comfort wear," like flip flops, runners, sweatpants, and baseball caps, which are anathema to the elegant Italians.

And finally, a word on fur. Italian women do not have the same reservations about wearing real fur as other cultures do. However, Gucci have done very well out of its collection of faux fur jackets and coats. Whether animal rights campaigns can influence the well-entrenched concept of *Bella Figura* remains to be seen.

Driving Etiquette:

A word of advice: You may want to think twice about driving a car in the major cities of Italy. Everything is within walking or biking distance anyway. The Italians are not known for their patience or love of rules. You'll see cars parked in no-parking zones, and you'll get honked at furiously just for sticking to the speed limit or, God forbid, stopping at a red light. Even if a car stops to let you walk across a pedestrian crossing, the other cars behind him may try to speed past the stopped vehicle. Friday and Saturday nights are by far the worst times to drive. The further south you go, the shorter the fuse and the more unruly, particularly in Naples and Sicily.

Safety Precautions:

The nature of crime in Italy is, by and large, petty theft. Bag snatching, pick-pocketing, passport theft, and theft from cars is common, particularly around major tourist attractions, railway stations, airports, and bus terminals, with the petty crime rate rising in the busy tourist season. Always keep your wits about you, and be vigilant with your belongings. Thieves will often create a diversion (e.g., pretending to ask for directions, throwing items on the floor or on their intended victim) and rob people when their attention is diverted.

Be vigilant when stopped in a car at traffic lights, rest stops, and service stations, where robberies frequently occur. There have been reports of thieves staging roadside emergencies, persuading drivers to pull over, and stealing their valuables while the passengers are distracted. Car break-ins and theft is also common. Always ensure valuables are never left in the car and that the car is locked when unattended, even for short periods.

Credit card fraud is also quite common, and involves "skimming" the machine that stores the credit card data. Only use ATMs in secure areas such as banks and shopping malls.

Never accept food or drink from a stranger, however genuine they may seem. Many have been robbed after drinking "spiked" beverages.

[eleven]
Japan

"Fall seven times and stand up eight."

– JAPANESE PROVERB

Historic Influences:

From evidence of pottery and clay figurines that date back 8,000 years, we know that the ancient Japanese lived as farmers and fishermen. It was in the period between 300AD–710AD that the ancient Japanese became heavily influenced by China. Learning to make paper, porcelain, silk and lacquer from the Chinese, they adopted the Chinese calendar and planned their cities in the Chinese way. During this time, the two religions, Shinto and Buddhism, co-existed peacefully.

However, from the year 646 a series of reforms stipulated that all land in Japan belonged to the emperor and that peasants had to pay taxes either in goods (e.g., rice and cloth), in labor, or by serving as soldiers. By the late 7th century, Japan saw rich landowners becoming increasingly powerful, employing private armies and warriors called *samurai*. Thus the fight for control over Japan by warring feudal lords began. In this age of absolute monarchy and dictatorship, even human life was governed by its rulers. With increasing friction, civil war finally broke out in 1180.

Finally, Ieyasu Tokugawa seized power for himself in 1603 and succeeded in unifying Japan under a strong central government. Called the Tokugawa shogunate, he was able to bring the feudal lords under his sway. Still a form of dictatorship, Tokugawa governed the country by his own law and Japanese society became strictly divided: feudal landlords were at the top of the hierarchy, followed by the samurai, farmers, craftsmen, and merchants.

In 1868, Japan fell into another civil war, with pro-emperor forces clashing against the pro-shogun side. The victor, Emperor Meiji, was determined to modernize Japan. In an astonishingly short period under his leadership, he transformed Japan from an agricultural nation to a modern industrialized power. The strict social pyramid collapsed forming a new system consisting of the Emperor, the aristocracy and the common people.

In the early stages of the 1900s, much of Japan's modern history was preoccupied with the fight for economic, political and military control. The Japanese people were obliged to work hard, lead frugal lives to build up the war funds, and display unwavering loyalty to the national cause, not dissimilar to feudal times.

After being brought down to its knees several times over the decades - during World War II, during its Great Recession in 1990, and throughout its various natural disasters - Japan has always managed to triumphantly rise from the ashes. Today, with its thriving population of 127 million, Japan's culture has evolved into a hybrid of Asian, European, and Western influences. And yet many of the intricacies that govern social etiquette in Japan are still characterized by an ancient, strict, and complex code of behavior that stems from Japan's feudal past. While the Japanese do not expect foreign visitors to be familiar with all their customs, they do expect them to behave formally and politely.

Religion In Japan:

Japan does not have a state religion. Shinto ritual is usually employed for births, whereas Buddhist ritual is preferred for deaths. Most Japanese follow both, and visit Shinto shrines and Buddhist temples.

The Japanese Concept of Face:

To understand the Japanese, we need to understand the concept of an honor-based society and "face." Face can be defined by a person's value, prestige, and standing in the eyes of their community. The thought of losing face to a Japanese is the equivalent of social death and is to be avoided at all cost.

The Japanese go out of their way to be polite and accommodating, avoiding disputes, conflicts and embarrassment in their pursuit to avoid losing face. As a foreigner in Japan, it is important to understand how face can be lost, earned, or taken away so that your Japanese host, associate, or friend does not lose face as a result of your actions or words. The triggers don't even have to be extreme.

While in the West it is normal to say a direct "no" in response to a request or question, you will almost never hear a Japanese utter a direct "no." A vague "yes" doesn't always mean "yes" either. Saying "no" to somebody directly, or contradicting somebody in front of anyone who is of a lower rank during a conversation, can cause that person to lose face. So if you need to give a negative reply to a Japanese, try saying something like, "maybe," "it's inconvenient," "it's under consideration," or even "this may be difficult."

Face can be lost, taken away, or earned through praise and thanks. For this reason one must always be gracious with one's praise and thanks in Japan. The Japanese also love to correspond, so a beautiful card or thank you note will go a long way. Sending your "thank you" via email would be considered insulting and lead to a loss of face for your host as it would imply their lack of importance.

While freedom of the individual is more important than group harmony in the West, the Japanese value civility, conformity, order, stability, and emphasis on obligations to the community or group. These values are generally shared by other Asian cultures, but especially the Chinese. People in the West are considered by the Japanese to have "thick" faces, as our verbal communication style is more direct and has little concern for non-verbal cues. People from the West are also more open when it comes to criticism. In Japan, criticism must be done very gently, accompanied with a lot of ego rubbing.

The Japanese trust non-verbal messages more than the spoken word, as words can have several meanings. For this reason, they maintain an impassive expression when speaking and rely heavily on facial expression, tone of voice, and posture. For example, frowning while someone is speaking is interpreted as a sign of disagreement. Other expressions to watch out for include inhaling through clenched teeth, tilting the head, scratching the back of the head, and scratching the eyebrow.

You may find that the Japanese may ask personal questions as a polite way to show their interest. Be cautious about disclosing information that you think may be too personal, or may cause your Japanese host or colleague discomfort. This may lead you to lose face with them, and they to lose face as a result of their association with you. Issues such as single motherhood, homosexuality, and/or divorce may fall in this category. Even though certain issues may be widely discussed and accepted in the West, remember that some parts of Japan, and some Japanese, are still very conservative.

Greeting & Conversation Etiquette:

Greetings in Japan are very formal and ritualized, which means that it is important to show the correct amount of respect and deference to someone based upon their status. Use the honorific suffix *san* when addressing all men and women; for instance Mr Yamada would be addressed as *Yamada-san*. Always wait to be introduced, even at a large gathering. It can be seen as impolite to introduce yourself. Make an effort to say a few basic words in Japanese - like "hello" (*konnichiwa*), "thank you" (*domo arigato*), "excuse me" (*sumimasen*), and "goodbye" (*sayonara*) - as it will be greatly appreciated.

In Japan, bowing is the customary greeting, although handshaking is becoming more common for business meetings with Westerners. Their handshakes tends to be limp with little or no eye contact so combine your handshake with a slight bow to show respect - you can read more on bowing at the end of this section.

Western people value eloquence and the art of persuasion. We tend to become uncomfortable with silences in our conversation and become desperate to fill in the gaps for fear of appearing inarticulate or uninformed. The opposite is true for the Japanese, who are suspicious of anyone who talks too much, a trait that they perceive as a way of taking advantage of others. The Japanese will use silence in negotiations to get what they want. So when in conversation with the Japanese, learn to become comfortable with silences and resist the temptation to fill the gaps with chatter. When listening to Japanese speak, nod your head to show that you are listening, and understand what the speaker is saying.

Last but not least, avoid the habit that some Westerners have of speaking louder when they think they are not being understood in Japan. Not only will this not get your message across any more effectively, it will cause great offense. The Japanese rarely raise their voices when speaking.

When and how to bow in Japan:

A bow can range from a small nod of the head to a long, 90 degree bend at the waist, depending on the seniority of the person you are bowing to. As well as a sign of greeting, a bow is used to express thanks, apologize, make a request, or to ask someone a favor.

- When bowing to someone of higher social status, a deeper, longer bow indicates respect.

- A small head nod is more casual and informal.

- If the greeting takes place on a tatami floor, people get on their knees in order to bow.

Conversation Taboos:

- Avoid bringing up the topics of World War II, the bombing of Hiroshima and Nagasaki, or Japan's connections and actions during the war. Bringing them up not only does not serve a purpose, it will cause your Japanese colleague or friend to lose face.

- Refrain from being critical about any aspect of the Japanese culture, or government, which you do not agree with. Criticism of Japan or the Japanese will cause a loss of face.

Appropriate Social Behavior:

In Japan, it is considered poor manners not to remove one's shoes before entering a home. This also applies to temples, some restaurants, and even some businesses. This custom was a practical necessity during times when roads were often wet and muddy, and to track mud into someone's home would have been a sign of disrespect. With time, this practice has become tradition.

The Japanese avoid eye contact as a means of giving themselves privacy. Staring into another person's eyes is, therefore, considered a gross invasion of privacy, particularly if the person is more senior to you, in which case it would show a lack of respect.

The Japanese rarely laugh or smile with strangers. However, because it is considered inappropriate to express embarrassment or sadness openly, the Japanese may laugh or smile when something bad has happened. Although this behavior may be considered odd in the West, a smile or laugh is a way for the Japanese to apologize or escape an uncomfortable situation without losing face. If you witness this type of behavior, do laugh or smile along with them as it means that you accept their apology, or you are joining with them in a sympathetic way.

The Japanese do not understand the Western concept of irony. Don't be surprised if your efforts at being clever or funny through irony or sarcasm is met with a blank stare and puzzlement.

Gift Giving Etiquette:

Gift giving is a very important part of Japanese culture. It's highly recommended that you bring a small and high-quality gift for your host that represents your native country, hometown, or company. The gift shows gratitude for your host's hospitality, and will always be appreciated. Avoid making the mistake of giving something that has "made in China" or "made in Japan" on the label. Also avoid giving gifts in quantities of four as this symbolizes death.

To the Japanese, a beautifully presented gift means that you are honoring the recipient of the gift. Therefore, presents should always be beautifully wrapped in either conservative wrapping paper or in a gift bag. Avoid wrapping the gift in red, black, or white, which are colors used for funerals.

Gifts should be given shortly after arriving at the home of your host and presented with both hands modestly. Even though the host may refuse it, insist that they receive it. You will more than likely be given a gift by your host when you arrive, so remember that gifts are received with both hands.

If the gift is wrapped, the correct etiquette is not to open it until you leave, or unless you are specifically asked to do so by the presenter. If the gift is not wrapped, make sure you are lavish with your appreciation and praise. You may even want to ask some questions about the gift to show interest.

Dining Etiquette:

"Living in Manila (Philippines) as a child, my father had invited a group of Japanese dignitaries to our home for dinner. Since part of the menu consisted of shellfish, a finger bowl filled with hot water and lemon was brought to each guest so that they could wash their hands after the course. Seeing the bowls in front of them, our Japanese guests gently lifted the bowl to their lips and drank from them. My father and mother, not missing a beat, did the same. When I asked my father afterwards why he didn't let our guests know that the bowl was for their hands, he explained that to do so would have only caused our Japanese guests to lose face."

- VICTORIA UGARTE, TRAVEL WRITER AND AUTHOR OF THIS BOOK.

Although a Japanese host will always be more tolerant towards a foreign visitor, do take the time to become familiar with basic dining etiquette in Japan, as it is generally more formal than in the West. Firstly, shoes should be removed before entering someone's home, with toes pointed out, making it easier to slip on when leaving. House slippers are provided for guests by the host at the doorway. It's appropriate to wear the slippers throughout the home, except in the bathroom (where special toilet slippers are provided) and the tatami floor of the dining room. Tatami should only be stepped on with socks or bare feet.

Sitting on the floor is common at mealtimes, during the tea ceremony, and other traditional events. The proper way to sit for both men and women is by kneeling and sitting back over one's feet, with the back upright. Foreigners may get uncomfortable after a while, and are not expected to be able to sit like this for hours. In more casual situations, men usually sit cross-legged while women may sit with both legs to one side.

The use of chopsticks is the most fundamental part of Japanese table manners, so *do* learn how to use them. Knives and forks are used for Western food only. Spoons, however, may be used with certain Japanese dishes, and a Chinese style ceramic spoon is sometimes provided for soups.

Here are some things to remember when eating with chopsticks:

- Hold your chopstick closer to the thicker end at the top, not in the middle or all the way towards the front (slimmer end).

- Never stick your chopsticks into your food, and especially not into the rice. The practice of sticking chopsticks into the rice is reserved for funerals, when rice is placed at the altar.

- Remember that your chopsticks are not a conductor's baton or magic wand that you wave around in the air while speaking, nor is it something that you spear food with, move bowls and plates around with, or drum on the tables.

- Passing food from your set of chopsticks to another's is a no-no, as this too is a funeral practice.

- When you're serving yourself food from shared dishes, use the opposite end of your chopsticks (thicker end) to move some food from the shared plates onto your own if you have not already eaten from your chopsticks. Otherwise, use the serving chopsticks that may be provided for that purpose.

- Do not drop your chopsticks, as it is considered bad luck.

When taking from a communal dish, it is important that you wait for your turn rather than serving yourself while another is still taking from the dish. The bones of the dead are lifted out of the cremation urn with four chopsticks, and it is for this reason why the older Japanese avoid more than one person taking from a dish at the same time.

When offered food, it is polite to hesitate before accepting. You do not have to eat much, but try a little bit of everything. It is quite acceptable to ask what something is. And I know it's acceptable in other Asian culture, but don't mix the other food with the rice while in Japan. It's not considered good dining etiquette.

Your soup should accompany your meal, so don't finish it before sampling the other dishes. Replace the lid of the soup bowl as soon as you have finished eating.

You are welcome to slurp your noodles and soup in Japan, as it shows that you're enjoying the meal. But draw the line at blowing your nose at the table or burping. This is considered very bad manners.

Empty your dish to the last grain of rice. It shows that you enjoyed your meal, you are complimenting your host, and that you do not want to waste any food. After eating, try to arrange your dishes back to the same position that they were in at the start of the meal, including replacing their lids and putting chopsticks back on the chopstick holder.

In Japan, it is customary to say *itadakimasu* ("I gratefully receive") before eating, and *gochisosama* (*deshita*) ("Thank you for the meal") after finishing the meal.

Etiquette For Guests At A Tea Ceremony:

"If man has no tea in him, he is incapable of understanding truth and beauty."

– JAPANESE PROVERB

To be invited to a Japanese tea ceremony is to be honored with one of Japan's most ancient customs. Influenced by Zen Buddhism, the ceremony requires strict adherence to rules that are designed to promote tranquility.

Always be prompt when arriving so that your host can begin the ceremony on time. After removing your shoes in the entryway of the home, step instantly onto the tatami room in your stockinged or slippered feet. This way, you avoid bringing whatever dirt there may be in the entryway of the home into the clean tatami room.

Once you have entered the tatami room, greet the guests who are already there with a slight bow, and sit down in the place indicated by your host. Stay in your place, be silent, and refrain from shaking hands with other guests.

You will be served a small cake on a small plate, called *o-kashi*. Pick up the plate with one hand and hold it at chest level, so that crumbs fall on the plate rather than on you or the tatami flooring. Eat the cake in several delicate bites, then put the plate back down gently in its original position. It is important that you eat everything that is served.

The tea will be served after you have eaten the *o-kashi*. Before you pick up your cup, bow to those guests who have not yet been served tea, pick up the cup with your right hand, bring it to chest level, and hold it there for a moment. Turn the bowl in two quarter turns in a clockwise direction, then drink the tea completely in several sips. The tea bowl is turned slightly so as to avoid drinking from the front side of the bowl. When your bowl is empty, turn the bowl back in the opposite direction in two quarter turns. Gently place the bowl down in its original position in front of you, on the tatami. Make a formal bow to your host to signal that you have finished drinking the tea and that you have set the bowl down.

Guests are served individually and in order of status in the Japanese tea ceremony. If there are others to be served, polite and gentle conversation with those still waiting, or have finished drinking, is acceptable. Being too loud or disruptive is considered rude as it disrupts the harmony of the ceremony. When everyone has been served, everyone makes a bow of gratitude to the host and then departs.

Each and every implement used in a Japanese tea ceremony has special significance, and has been thoughtfully selected. Treat them with respect and compliment your host on them with great sincerity. After two days, send your host a handwritten note, or make a phone call to express your appreciation for the invitation.

Social Drinking Etiquette:

Social drinking is big in Japan as it's a way to cope with the stress from having to continually avoid confrontation and suppress anger for the sake of social harmony. In fact, the Japanese do not even regard alcohol as a drug. Breaking down the strict social barriers, host and guests take turns filling each other's cups and encouraging each other to gulp it down.

When drinking alcoholic beverages it is customary for the Japanese to serve each other rather than themselves. It's considered polite to check your friends' cups every so often and refill their drinks if you see that their cups need topping up. If someone wants to serve you more alcohol, quickly empty your glass then hold your glass towards that person with both hands.

While it is considered bad manners to get drunk in more formal restaurants, it is acceptable in the more casual bar/restaurants in Japan called *izakaya,* so long as you do not bother other guests. However, it's not considered good manners to start drinking until everybody at the table is served, and glasses are raised for a toast. The appropriate toast in Japan is *kampai.* Whatever you do, avoid using the words *chin chin* when drinking a toast since in Japanese this refers to the male genitalia.

If you do not want anything more to drink, do not finish what is in your glass. An empty glass is an invitation for someone to serve you more.

Saying 'No' To Alcohol In Japan:

It can be difficult escaping the ritual of the social drink in Japan if you do not drink alcohol. The easiest way is to just apologise by saying *gomennasai, alcohoru nomemasen.* This means "I'm sorry, I cannot drink alcohol." Although it is normally impolite to refuse anything in Japan, this is considered acceptable because you have started your sentence with an apology

Dressing Etiquette:

The Japanese pride themselves on their appearance and are known for being impeccably dressed and groomed. Their style is a blend of modern and conservative, with a preference for designer labels that are not showy or revealing. To be appropriately dressed in Japan, steer yourself towards a simple, neat, and well-groomed look.

Dress smartly for parties or a dinner invitation, even if the occasion says "casual." For business and dinner invitations, women should wear dresses with pantyhose, blouse and skirt, or a suit. Shoes should have a slight heel. You may want to choose more subtle colors and conservative styles for a business meeting. As with other countries of the world, always dress modestly when visiting a temple or shrine.

Bathing Etiquette:

The Japanese value neatness and cleanliness as it aligns with their sense of order. The act of bathing is extremely important to their culture. Besides cleaning the body, the main purpose of having a bath is to relax and clear the mind at the end of the day.

The typical Japanese bathroom consists of two rooms, an entrance room where you undress, and the actual bathroom, which is equipped with a shower and a deep bath tub. Toilets are separate to the bathrooms. It's important that you leave the normal house slippers outside the door of the toilet/ bathroom and use the special bathroom slippers that are provided.

Here is how the Japanese go about their bathing:

- Firstly, they rinse the body outside the bath tub with the washbowl provided, or with the shower head, in order to cleanse the body thoroughly.

- Secondly, they enter the tub filled with hot water (no bubbles or essential oils), which is used for soaking only. The bath water tends to be relatively hot by Western bathing standards.

- Thirdly, after a good soaking, they leave the tub and soap the body thoroughly, making sure that no soap gets into the bathing water, as the same bath water will be used by all members of the household.

- Finally, they rinse all the soap off the body before re-entering the bath tub for a final soaking.

If you are staying with a Japanese family in their home, remember that bathing takes place in the evenings. Guests are expected to bathe first, followed by children, the female head of the household, and the male head of the household. You may want to forget about sneaking in a bath in the mornings as the bathing area is normally used for laundry during the day, and you'll end up throwing your host's day out by having that morning bath.

If the thought of the bath water being re-used by several family members after you makes you uncomfortable, then just skip the soak altogether and have a quick shower outside of the bath. No one will be watching you anyway.

Japanese Temple Etiquette:

There are several types of temples in Japan; the family temples, and the larger temples and shrines.

Each family has an established family temple and burial ground related to a specific Buddhist sect. You can usually tell if a particular temple is geared towards families if the temple is empty of visitors, or if there is an old lady in the cemetery surrounding the temple, looking after the tombs. There is not much else for you to do in family temples than visit the cemetery, so be respectful of the tombs, maintain silence, and do not touch anything.

When visiting a large temple or shrine, do not do anything you would not do in a church, temple, or synagogue. Make sure you are dressed and behave modestly and respectfully. There usually is an entrance fee to be paid prior to entering a temple, with brochures explaining the history. Ask if there is an English version if you do not speak Japanese. While photography is usually permitted on the temple grounds, chances are it will be forbidden inside, so watch out for the signs.

Upon entering the temple, you'll find a stone basin usually covered by a roof, with a bamboo pipe sprouting water. This is so that visitors can wash themselves before entering the sanctuary of the temple; using the ladle, rinse your right hand with a little water, making sure that the water falls on the ground and not back into the basin. Then change hands and rinse the left hand. After washing your hands, cup your right hand and pour a little water in it to rinse your mouth, spitting the water discreetly on the ground. Do not drink from the ladle. Finally, hold the ladle vertically to let the rest of the contents pour down the handle to purify it for the next person and place it back on the stand in the basin. There will be a towel hanging around the basin for drying your hands.

Keep an eye out for what the shoe etiquette is at the particular temple you are visiting. There is sometimes a shelf where you can leave your shoes before entering. Alternatively, an attendant might hand you a plastic bag to carry your shoes in, particularly if you will be exiting from another area of the temple.

Next, you will more than likely have to step over a raised threshold before entering the main body of the temple. Be mindful not to step on it, but over it. It is highly disrespectful to step on the threshold. Before entering, uncover your head if you're wearing a hat or cap. Bow towards the main idol or altar as a sign of respect when you get inside.

Once inside the temple, don't pass in front of someone who is praying, no matter how far they are from the altar or idol. It is considered disrespectful.

In front of the main altar, there may be a bell at the end of a long rope hanging from the ceiling. You can throw money in the collection box and then ring the bell. After ringing the bell, clap your hands twice, bow once and pray silently. The clapping is said to attract the attention of the gods. When you are done praying, bow again, clap your hands once, and back away from the place. If there is no bell in front of the altar, do not clap your hands. Just join your hands at chest level, using the universal sign for prayer, and pray silently.

At some temples, you can purchase incense to burn in large incense burners, a ritual that is said to have great healing powers. After lighting the incense and letting it burn for a few seconds, extinguish the flame by waving your hand rather than by blowing the flame out. After positioning the incense into the incense burner, fan some smoke towards yourself.

When leaving the temple, turn toward the altar at the door and bow once as a sign of respect.

Toilet Etiquette:

There are two types of toilets in Japan: Japanese style and Western style. While public washrooms are often equipped with both toilet styles, some older facilities might have only Japanese style toilets. The toilets in most public homes and hotels are generally Western style.

Before we start on the actual toilets, remember that there are special toilet slippers for exclusive use inside the toilet/ bathroom/ washroom. Make sure that you leave your house slippers outside the washroom/toilet door and use the toilet slippers provided before entering. You'll need to balance your body as you swap the house slippers for the toilet slippers, making sure that your feet don't touch the floor and the toilet slippers don't touch the floor beyond the washroom. Don't forget to swap slippers again on your way out.

In this land of high-tech gadgetry, the Western style toilets in Japan feature a mind boggling array of bells and whistles, such as a heated seat ring, a built-in shower, dryer for your behind, and an automatic lid opener. If you're lucky, you might get some music thrown in, although I have yet to sit on one that speaks (as their elevators do). The toilet options are there to assure that everyone's needs, and hygiene habits, are taken care of.

If you're really confused as to what buttons to press in the Japanese toilets, may I suggest that you avoid pressing any buttons altogether, unless you don't mind an unexpected surprise. If you're not into adventure of the toilet variety, may I suggest you stick to the two flush modes, which refers to the amount of water in the flush.

- Small flush - (小)

- Large flush - (大)

Toilet paper is not always provided in public washrooms in Japan, so always carry a small packet of tissues in your handbag. Some Japanese toilets have a water reserve above the toilet tank so when it's flushed, guests can rinse their hands.

As for the traditional Japanese toilets, they are a little trickier to negotiate for Westerners. Built into the floor, using them requires a little more flexibility. Here's how to use them: face the front of the toilet, pull down your trousers/skirt completely below your knees, and squat down as closely to the front of the toilet as possible. If the edges are elevated, you'll need to stand on the raised platform while squatting. And pray like hell that your balance holds.

Safety Precautions:

Japan is subject to volcanic activity, earthquakes, tsunamis and typhoons. An earthquake on 11 March 2011, and the subsequent tsunami, caused significant damage to areas along the northeast coast of Japan, resulting in significant casualties. One must always check official travel bulletins regarding weather and climate patterns prior to visiting Japan.

Although the crime rate in Japan is relatively low, credit card and ATM fraud can occur. Be cautious of any machines that have items stuck to them or look unusual.

There have been reports of drink spiking at bars and various entertainment venues, with the purpose of assault or stealing credit cards. When possible, avoid carrying credit cards when visiting bars and nightclubs.

There have been sporadic incidents of bag snatching and the pick-pocketing of foreigners in crowded areas such as shopping centers, trains, and airports. Be extra alert in these areas.

twelve

Latin America

"And one by one the nights between our separated cities are joined to the night that unites us."

– PABLO NERUDA, CHILEAN POET AND POLITICIAN.

Historic Influences:

Latin America is the land of the tango, salsa, merenge, and reggaetón, where rhythm is in the air and passion is in the bones. It's history spans a large range of cultural forms. The first evidence of civilization and existence of agricultural practices in South America dates back to c 6500 BC, when potatoes, chilies and beans were cultivated for food in the Amazon Basin. Llamas and alpacas started to be domesticated for transportation, meat, and clothing as early as 3500 BC in the Andes highlands. By 2000 BC, village communities had begun to scatter throughout the Andes and surrounding regions. Fishing and irrigation greatly aided the rise of these communities.

Prior to the arrival of the Europeans, an estimated 30 million inhabitants lived in permanent settlements throughout South America. These settlements were comprised of the Cañaris, the indigenous natives of Ecuador, the Chibchas, the most socio-economically developed society of the Pre-Hispanic Colombians, the hunter-gatherer settlements around the Amazon, and the Andean civilizations, dominated by the Incas.

In 1493, a papal bull (or charter issued by the Pope of the Catholic Church) gave Portugal and Spain permission to take possession of non-Christian lands and encouraged the enslavement of the non-Christian people of Africa and the Americas. After signing the Treaty of Tordesilhas, the two maritime powers agreed that all land outside Europe be an exclusive duopoly between the two. They proceeded to divide the lands between themselves, exploit the people, and claim the natural resources as their own. With a commitment to converting their subjects to Christianity, the Spaniards very quickly purged any native practices that were contrary to this end. After a while, the Spaniards and natives interbred, which formed the beginnings of the mestizo class. This word is still used to this day.

Through the trans-Atlantic slave trade, South America, particularly Brazil, became the new settlement for the Africans who were enslaved and shipped to the Americas. The tensions between the European colonizers, the indigenous population, and the African slaves, shaped South America from the 16th–19th centuries.

The revolution for independence from the Spanish monarchy during the 19th century saw South America undergoing more social and political changes. Several factors produced conflict that stretched out until the early 1900s and carved a permanent mark on the local psyche: waves of European immigration, increased trade, the colonization of the inland areas, reorganization of indigenous rights, and preoccupation with the power balance.

During the Cold War and the late 20th century, South America once again became a battlefield for the superpowers, with the governments of Argentina, Brazil, Chile and Uruguay being overthrown or displaced by US-aligned dictatorships. By the 1980s, however, a wave of democratization spread throughout the continent. Although allegations of corruption remain, and international indebtedness became a big problem, democratic rule is now widespread. South America, and in particular Brazil, is now enjoying its best years of economic growth.

Definitions of Latin America may vary, but from a cultural perspective, it includes the parts of the Americas where a predominant language holds sway:

- Spanish - Argentina, Belize, Bolivia, Brazil, Chile, Colombia, Costa Rica, Dominican Republic, Ecuador, El Salvador, Guatemala, Honduras, Nicaragua, Mexico, Peru, Venezuela.

- Portuguese - Brazil.

A major characteristic of Latin American culture is that it is predominantly patriarchal. Rigid divisions exist between work and home, with Latin men and women polar opposites of each other, their complementary roles forming the foundations of Latin American society. In this part of the world, the stereotypes are strong, with little room for seemingly passive men or aggressive women.

Greeting & Conversation Etiquette:

In Latin America, men shake hands with each other when meeting and departing. When shaking hands with a woman, a man allows the woman to extend her hand first. Handshaking is firm but brief, with direct eye contact maintained throughout the handshake.

To kiss or not to kiss. In casual situations, women and women, as well as men and women, kiss each other on the cheek when greeting. The number of times, and which side of the face, one should kiss varies according to the region. Just observe and you'll figure it out soon enough. However, kissing a stranger is considered impolite, particularly when you are in a business gathering, and especially if the person is an elder.

Unlike the Arabs, Latin men never kiss each other, unless they are grandfather and grandson, father and son, or brothers. However, Latin men frequently hug each other and give each other backslaps if they are really close friends.

Children play a very large part in the Latin American culture, with children being taught from an early age how to be sociable and polite. They are usually prompted by their parent to greet everyone in their parent's social circle, so don't forget to greet the children if they are present at a social engagement.

The courtesy titles of *Señor, Señora* and *Señorita* mean Mr, Mrs and Miss, respectively. Greeting someone with *Hola* (hello) is always followed by the appropriate time of day greeting and their courtesy title: *buenos dias* (good day), *buenas tardes* (good afternoon), and *buenas noches* (good evening). The elderly are given high respect in Latin America. Men are often referred to as *Don* and women as *Doña*, followed by their first names.

Titles are also important in Latin America. Address a person directly by using his or her title only. A Ph.D. or a physician is called *Doctor,* teachers are called *Profesor,* engineers go by *Ingeniero,* architects are *Arquitecto,* and lawyers are *Abogado.* Persons who do not have professional titles should be addressed by their Spanish courtesy titles of Mr, Mrs, or Miss.

Saying goodbye is said in two popular ways in Latin America, *Adios* and *Chau* (derived from the Italian word *ciao*). Like the French, group waves for saying "hello" or "goodbye" are unacceptable, so take the time to say hello and goodbye to each person separately in a group.

People in the center regions of Latin America may be sensitive to the use of formal and informal Spanish. For example in a business meeting, it would be more appropriate to use *usted*, the formal word for "you" rather than *tu*. The more informal *tu* is reserved for people that you are on a first name basis with, in a more casual environment.

Among Latin Americans, the conversations are usually lively and full of interruptions. If you're talking to someone else and a third person joins you, do stop what you're saying and acknowledge the newcomer. If two or more people are having a conversation and you need to leave, you can excuse yourself by saying *disculpe* (excuse me) or *con permiso* (with your permission).

When someone sneezes, you should respond with *salud* (meaning "health"). The person who sneezed should respond with *gracias* (thank you).

Show respect for the native peoples of Latin America by referring to them as *indígenas*, literally meaning "indigenous people." The term *indios* (Indians) is a derogatory term.

Remember that Brazilians speak Portuguese, not Spanish. Although most Brazilians understand Spanish reasonably well, some may be offended if you initially address them in Spanish without attempting a few words in Portuguese first. Make it a point to learn some basic Portuguese before traveling to Brazil. Your efforts will be welcomed.

Conversation Taboos:

- Most Latin Americans will let you know what they want to converse about, so let them take the lead. However, it is never a good idea to ask questions about personal finances or gains, or ask a woman her age in Latin America.

- Critical comments about the country, volatile political history, or corruption within the government by foreign guests are taboo, even though the criticism may be true.

- Familiarize yourself with the current affairs of countries like Guatemala, El Salvador, Colombia, Chile, Nicaragua, or Peru, before traveling there. Refrain from discussing the past political history of the country if it has not been a favorable one.

- In Argentina, avoid discussing the Peron years, religion and the Falkland Islands conflict.

- In Chile, avoid discussion about politics, particularly Pinochet and the country's history with civil unrest.

- In Colombia, bullfighting is considered a national pastime, so avoid expressing your disapproval or getting into an ethics debate over it.

- Avoid at all cost discussions regarding the drug trade. It seems to be the first question that every foreign guest asks a Colombian, and the people of Colombia do take exception to this.

- In the Dominican Republic, avoid discussing Haitian immigration, Dominican emigration, and racial identity, where most of the population are mixed-race African/ Caucasian.

- In Mexico, avoid discussions on the national differences between US and Mexico, racial/ethnic issues, or global diplomatic issues.

Appropriate Social Behavior:

"Laughter is the language of the soul."

- PABLO NERUDA, CHILEAN POET, DIPLOMAT AND POLITICIAN.

Latin Americans demonstrate a more relaxed/casual behavior in comparison to much of the English speaking world. They are comfortable with loud talk, exaggerated gestures, physical contact and showing of affection.

Gender specific behavior by men towards women in Latin America is considered good manners and not flirtatious at all (e.g., opening the door, lighting a cigarette, giving a woman a seat, pulling the chair out for her, or helping her with her luggage). It is also common for Latino men to stare at women, or even bombard them with catcalls. Unlike other countries where such expressions can be considered as aggressive sexual advances, in Latin America it is considered harmless behavior that is meant to flatter the woman. Having said this, women may not respond in kind and should be especially careful about making any glances or gestures that might be considered overtly flirtatious.

In keeping with the relaxed behavior trend, punctuality is not taken too seriously in Latin America. Unlike the Germans and Swedes, showing up exactly on schedule for a party is not common. However, punctuality is always expected in business.

Many Latin Americans have a smaller sense of personal space than people from northern Europe or the West. They tend to stand closer to one another when talking to each other or when standing in queues (lines). Avoid stepping away when some-one attempts to step closer in conversation as your gesture may be considered a rejection of their company. And visitors from Australia, Great Britain and the US take note: Latin Americans do not recognize, let alone follow, queue etiquette (standing in line).

Before dropping by someone's home, ensure that you call first to ask that it is convenient. If they offer you snacks or something to drink when you drop by, it is often polite to decline the first time, but to accept after they insist. To refuse still after they insist would be considered rude.

As is the case with many Eastern and Western cultures, it is considered rude to point at a person or even an object with the index finger. In Latin America, people typically point with the whole hand, or with a movement of the head and a puckering of the lips, towards the object or person that is being indicated. It is also considered impolite to "toss" objects at people instead of directly handing it to them.

The concept of honor and personal pride go hand-in-hand with Latin America's patriarchal society, so highlighting someone's shortcomings in front of others is not a great idea. Even though Latin Americans tend to be more direct in social situations, they are surprisingly subtle when it comes to making requests and offering criticism. Make sure that indiscretions and errors are pointed out in private, never in front of other people, particularly in a business environment, or risk the person feeling humiliated and responding with hostility.

Salsa, merengue, reggaetón, and tango may all seem like "sexy dancing" to foreigners, but it is still considered improper for a man to dance too close to a woman who is not his wife or girlfriend.

When smoking, offer a cigarette to everyone. Cover your mouth when yawning or coughing, and never eat or blow your nose in public. All these behaviors are considered to be rude.

There are certain gestures that are commonly used in Western cultures that would not be well received in Latin America, so cool it with the non-verbal gestures. The American "come here" gesture of palm upwards with the fingers curled back can be considered a romantic or sexual solicitation. In Brazil, the American "OK" gesture, by connecting the thumb and forefinger in a circle, is considered obscene as it depicts a certain part of the anatomy (the "thumbs up" version of 'OK' is acceptable). And two pointing fingers as Americans would use to indicate length is also an obscene gesture in Colombia.

The Indigenous population:

While the majority of Latin Americans are warm and relaxed, the same does not apply to many of the Indigenous population. Andean people, for example, are not very tactile with members of the opposite sex. Friends of the same sex may hold hands, shake hands, and even hold each other by the shoulder, and cheek-kissing between women is also acceptable. But any public display of affection between a couple, even holding hands, is done with awkwardness.

Many Indigenous people from small villages are reluctant to look a stranger in the eye, so respect their personal space and avoid direct eye contact with them. Similarly, avoid photographing any indigenous person without their express permission. If given permission, give them some money in return for the privilege.

Gift Giving Etiquette:

In Latin America, it is considered rude to show up to someone's home empty-handed. A small ornament for your host's home is acceptable if you are familiar with their decorative style. Otherwise, flowers, wine, chocolates, or a small toy or candies for the host's child are other good gift ideas. Gifts are never opened in front of a group of people unless the giver insists, so as to avoid people comparing the merits of different gifts.

Unless the gift is for a birthday, be cautious about giving a gift to the opposite gender as it may be misinterpreted as a romantic gesture. Also be careful about overly praising something in someone's home, or you could end up receiving it as a gift. In more rural areas, the practice of giving away objects that a visitor likes is considered the polite thing to do.

If bringing flowers, you may want to avoid the color purple. In parts of Latin America (e.g., Mexico) it is associated with funerals in the Catholic tradition.

For an informal lunch visit, it is common to bring a good-quality wine or liquor for the man of the house, and a dessert for the lady of the house. For breakfast, white cheese or shredded beef for the *arepa** is always welcome.

* *Arepa* is a bread made of corn originating from the northeast of Venezuela.

Dining Etiquette:

If dining and food is considered almost a religious experience in Latin America, then being invited for Sunday lunch in someone's home is the equivalent of High Mass. Sunday, usually after church, is the day Latin Americans reserve for a family meal and get together. An invitation to Sunday lunch, or dinner, signifies that your host holds you in high enough regard to include you with their family.

Table manners are Continental, meaning that all food is eaten with the fork held in the left hand and the knife in the right. There are several kinds of food from Mexico that may be eaten with the fingers, such as *tacos, tortas, churros* (Mexico). Eating them with a fork and knife is considered pretentious and comical. When in doubt, just follow the lead of the other diners. When it comes to finger food and appetizers, avoid picking up the last morsel on the plate without offering it around first. You will be considered uneducated and greedy.

Do not begin eating until the hostess invites you to do so, and wait for a toast to be made before taking the first sip of your drink. When eating in company, never put your hands under the table.

Refusing a second helping is a sign that you haven't enjoyed the food. But what is worse than refusing a second helping is eating very little because you're on a diet. At the very least, you will be told that you can continue your diet the following day. At worst, you will greatly offend your host.

Withdrawing from the table halfway through the meal is not acceptable, so don't even think about leaving the table to go to the bathroom or worse, to have a cigarette. Should your mobile phone ring, ignore it or switch it off for the remainder of the get-together.

When you have finished eating in company, even strangers, you must say *buen provecho* or *que aproveche* (good eating). This is answered with *gracias* (thank you). *Do* stay and socialize for a few hours after finishing your meal. Otherwise, your host may feel that you were there only for a free feed.

It is common for some Latin Americans, particularly of the Andean culture, to belittle and apologize for the food that they are serving. This is done to show politeness and humility. This is your cue to compliment your host for their hospitality and excellent offering.

If it's you who is doing the hosting in a rural setting, you need to serve the food to your guest and insist that they eat. Putting a plate in the middle of the table for people to help themselves, even if it's finger food, may create some awkwardness. Guests are usually served a plate and left alone to eat, unless you are considered a close friend or member of the family.

In some rural areas of Latin America, where doors may not have doorbells, either stand in the yard and clap your hands, or approach the door, knock, and then step back away from the door and await a response.

Business dinners are popular in Latin America and are usually held in restaurants rather than at homes; business lunches are less common outside of the major cities, since most people go home to eat lunch. When an invitation is issued for a restaurant or bar, it is assumed that everything will be paid for by the one inviting.

South American Barbecues:

While Aussies have their *barbies,* and South Africans have their *braaivleis,* the Argentinians have their *parillas* (pronounced pa-RI-LYAS). Traditionally a male domain, the ritual of the *parilla* is sacred to the Argentinians. A simple structure made up of a concrete floor, metal grill, and brick pyramid, the science consists of burning wood down to glowing embers before slow cooking huge racks of ribs, chorizos and steaks, carefully salting it with "*parilla* grade" sea salt especially made for the task. It doesn't take long for the air to be permeated with rosemary-flavored smoke and the mouthwatering aroma of cooking meat. When ready to eat, the meat is tender, smoky, and amazingly good.

Parillas are by and large casual affairs, where family and good friends gather together to enjoy good food, wine, and conversation. Here are some basic etiquette tips:

- Leave the cooking to the men, as this is their domain. Never tell them how your meat should be cooked, which would be nothing short of insulting.

- Should you be vegetarian, let your host know way ahead of time so that adequate preparations can be made.

- If you are vegetarian, be prepared for some good natured ribbing when you get there. After all, Argentina is known as the home of the steak.

- In Brazil, barbecues are known as *churrasco,* and the restaurants that specialize in this type of grilling are called *churrascarias.* Different cuts of all-you-can-eat meat are served to you at your table by waiters carrying skewers. This is usually enjoyed with an ice cold beer.

- If you are vegetarian, you may want to skip the *churrascaria* as this is a "meat only" establishment.

Hope For The Vegetarian:

While India is vegetarian heaven, South America will definitely test your resolve. In this continent of carnivores, there isn't much choice apart from your regular croissants, pastas, pizza, and cheese empanadas. The more out-of-town you go, the more limited the selection. Vegans will have even bigger problems, as most of the vegetarian options in South America contain cheese. To be able to explain your dietary requirements, you're going to have to learn phrases like *Soy vegetariana* in Spanish or *Eu sou um vegetarian* in Portuguese (translates to "I am vegetarian").

When in Argentina, you may want to try *Humitas* (pronounced OO-mi-tas), which is a snack made up of fresh corn and cheese mixed together with onion, wrapped up in a corn husk and boiled before serving. Remember not to eat the husk.

Quinoa is a grain-like food that originates from the Andean region of South America, and is quite common on menus in the higher altitude towns. It makes a great alternative to pasta, so look out for it in veg-only combinations.

Chipa is a cheese corn bread that is found everywhere in Paraguay, while *Mbeju,* a traditional starch pancake filled with cheese and melted over a fire, can often be found in festivals.

Bori-bori soup with corn dumplings is an indigenous specialty of Paraguay, but make sure that you confirm that it does not contain meat.

Mandioca is a potato-like root that can also be known as cassava or tapioca, and is in plentiful supply. It is delicious when eaten fried.

Self catering is by far the best option when the monotonous vegetarian selection in food stalls and restaurants starts to get to you. Keep your eyes peeled at the markets, where you can purchase a wide variety of fruit, dried snacks, vegetables, beans, lentils, and spices.

A tip for vegetarians:

> A useful thing to have is a discount resource guide for the vegetarian restaurants and food stores around South America Called *Golden Pages of the Original Kingdom,* just click on this link. It will give you names, addresses, as well as discounts. You can thank me later! www.thegoldenpages.info

Dressing Etiquette:

In a continent where women are polar opposites of their men, *Latina* women, particularly from the capital cities, ensure that they leave their homes beautifully dressed and impeccably groomed. Unless you want to have "foreign tourist" stamped across your forehead, avoid wearing sweat pants, runners, flip-flops, or anything better suited to a gym, beach, or resort. When going out at night, it is expected for a woman to dress fashionably and look her best.

If you wanted to dress in the traditional/ indigenous attire of the country, save it until you arrive back in your home country, where at least people will see you as "exotic." In Latin America, you'll only be seen as a silly tourist.

Always dress modestly when visiting churches and monasteries. Avoid wearing clothes that reveal a lot of skin (e.g., low-rise pants, midriff shirts, peek-a-boo thongs, and low cut tops). Skirts must cover the knees and T-shirts and tops must cover your chest and the tops of your arms. This means no singlets, ladies.

There's no delicate way to put this, but people's hygiene habits are very important in Latin America, especially in the tropical regions where people sweat. Women and men are expected to shower daily, often several times a day, and dress neatly. Body odor, unshaven legs and underarms in women, un-pedicured or dirty feet, wrinkled and soiled clothing, and dirty shoes, are considered disgusting by Latin Americans.

Safety Precautions:

Safety precautions differ between regions in South America, with different degrees of volatility, so always ensure that you look up government updates on the current political situations in each region before traveling there.

Pick-pocketing, bag snatching and bag slitting in crowded areas, like major tourist areas, or on public transport, can be a problem in South America. Exercise caution and be vigilant with your possessions.

Tourists have been the victims of armed robbery in some areas, particularly around isolated areas (e.g., traveling at night) and the archeological sites. It is advisable that you use a reputable tour company when organizing your tours. I also strongly recommend against traveling alone, as this leaves you vulnerable to harassment and sexual assault.

Take great care in festivals, such as Carnaval in Brazil, where criminals target tourists. Always dress down, avoid wearing expensive jewelry or watches, and travel in groups. If you are held up at knife or gunpoint, never resist. This can lead to serious injury or the loss of your life.

Tourists should stay away from the *favelas* or shanty towns, where the crime levels are high. Organized criminal gangs also target the beaches, particularly in the early evenings, so avoid isolated areas in the beach or going there at dusk.

Only use ATMs that are located in highly protected areas like shopping centers, or in secured sections within banks. "Express kidnappings" occur in some areas of South America, where victims are abducted and forced to withdraw funds from ATMs in order to secure their release.

Criminals also pose as taxi operators or taxi drivers, so make sure that you use only licensed taxis, and get into taxis at official ranks only, like major hotels. When in a vehicle, keep all windows closed and doors locked as carjackings are common in some areas. Do not travel in a taxi on your own, and do not allow the driver to pick up any additional passengers.

You can usually prepay your taxi fare just outside the terminals at airports, bus or train stations. You can also catch official taxis at the hotels. When eating out at restaurants, ask the restaurant manager to call you a taxi rather than hailing them from the street.

Avoid leaving food unattended, or accepting food, chewing gum, beverages, or cigarettes, from strangers. Thieves have been known to spray chemicals on these items to incapacitate their victims in some areas. This can occur in bars, public transport, restaurants, and cafés. Never accept paper handouts on the street, which can also be sprayed with a toxic chemical that causes serious harm when it touches your face, via your hands. Do not accept food or beverages from strangers in bars and nightclubs.

Protests and demonstrations are frequent in some areas of South America. It is best to avoid any public demonstrations or large gatherings as they may turn violent at a moment's notice.

Tourists traveling from the airport to the city are often targeted for theft. Keep all valuables hidden, including cameras and laptops. Never accept unsolicited help from strangers, and do not leave luggage unattended.

Highway robberies, followed by violence, occur frequently in Guatemala, including inter-city buses and luxury coaches in tourist areas or near border crossings. Crime levels have increased, particularly near the border of Guatemala and Mexico, due to drug trafficking and illegal immigration, so it is important that you cross Guatemala's borders during daylight hours.

Travelers in Peru who ascend to altitudes greater than 2,500m, for example Cuzco, Machu Picchu, Puno, and Lake Titicaca, are at risk of developing altitude sickness.

thirteen

Muslim Nations Of The Middle East

"Sunshine all the time makes a desert."

– ARAB PROVERB.

Historic Influences:

The earliest civilization in the world, said to have begun around 3500 BC, stems from the Middle East, with Mesopotamia (Iraq today) generally regarded as the cradle of civilization. The 6th century onwards saw the area being dominated by some of the greatest empires in history, beginning with the Persian empire, ruled by Achaemenids, followed by the Macedonians, led by Alexander the Great.

By the 1st century BC, the Roman empire had absorbed the whole Eastern Mediterranean area, uniting the East with Europe and North Africa. Known as the Byzantine Empire, and controlled from Constantinople, its cities became rich melting pots of culture, learning, and trade. Christianity spread until it became the dominant religion in the empire. In time, however, the rift between Constantinople and the rest of the Middle East began to widen, paving the way for Islam.

The 7th century onwards saw the force of Islam rising in the Middle East, with Arab armies, led by Caliphs and skilled military commanders, sweeping through the Middle East, reducing Byzantine lands by half and engulfing the Persian lands. The Arab Empire was the first empire to control the entire Middle East, three-quarters of the Mediterranean region, and most of the Mediterranean Sea. This is the dominant ethnic identity in the Middle East that we see today.

By the phrase "Muslim Nations of the Middle East," I refer to the following group of nations situated in the Middle East and Northern Africa, whose culture is predominantly Islamic: Afghanistan, Egypt, Iran, Iraq, Jordan, Lebanon, Libya, Morocco, Oman, Qatar, United Arab Emirates (UAE), and Yemen. By "culture is predominantly Islamic," I refer to the customs and traditions that Muslims have adopted, which include appropriate dress and codes of behavior as dictated by the *Qur'an*.

Islam, which began in Saudi Arabia, follows the teachings of the Prophet Muhammad, who is seen as the last of God's emissaries (after Jesus, Moses, Abraham, etc). As Moses brought the *Torah* and Jesus the *Bible,* Muhammad brought the last book, the *Qur'an* (*Koran*). The *Qur'an,* and the actions and sayings of the Prophet Muhammad, are used as the basis for all guidance in Islam, prescribing a way of life that governs political, legal, and social behavior for both society and the individual.

Facts About Arabs, Islam & the Role of Women:

Let us start this section by clearing up some popular misconceptions:

- Muslims must not be confused with Arabs. Muslims may be Arabs, but they can also be Turks, Persians, Indians, Pakistanis, Malaysians, Indonesians, Europeans, Africans, Americans, Chinese, and other nationalities.

- Only 12% of the world's Muslims are Arabs. Turkey and Iran, not Arab countries, are the most populous Muslim nations in the Middle East.

- Egypt, not Saudi Arabia, is the most populous Arab Muslim nation.

Muslim Women In The Middle East:

The social code for Muslim women in the Middle East has been the subject of much controversy, with all Muslim women being lumped into the category of oppressed creatures. While many of the more conservative nations in the Middle East have been ruled by governments that have been subject to religious authority, and that have sustained a largely patriarchal social framework, political reform is steadily bringing about different interpretations of the role of women in Middle Eastern society.

Having said that, in comparison to the West, the privacy of women in Middle Eastern society is highly protected. Men and women normally have different living areas in the home. Men and women are generally expected to socialize with members of their own sex. The extent, of course, varies from country to country, with the most restrictive conditions existing in the Arabian Peninsula. The urban areas of Egypt, Syria, and Lebanon are more relaxed and liberal. However, this situation may change at any time, depending on whether the power of government sways back towards a more patriarchal framework imposed by religious authority.

Rules of Prayer and of Ramadan:

Muslims are obliged to pray five times a day – at dawn, noon, afternoon, sunset, and evening. The exact times are listed in the local newspaper each day. Nearly every hotel room in the Arab world will have a decal stuck to the mirror, night table, or ceiling, showing Muslims the direction of Mecca, which they should face to pray. Friday is the Muslim holy day, and for this reason, all businesses are closed. Many companies close on Thursdays, making the weekend Thursday and Friday rather than Saturday and Sunday.

Prayer is called *Salat*. In Saudi Arabia everything shuts down during *Salat*. As a Westerner visiting a conservative Islamic country, it is wise to stop what you are doing and be respectful of the *Salat*. If indoors, stay there until the *Salat* is complete. If you must be out and about, refrain from standing directly in front of any Muslim in a prayer position.

Ramadan is the name of the ninth month in the Islamic calendar, and is a month of fasting. All Muslims must fast from dawn to dusk and are only permitted to work six hours per day. Fasting includes no eating, drinking, cigarette smoking, or gum chewing. Although Western guests are not required to fast, they must not eat, drink, smoke, or chew gum in public. This is a very important law and completely non-negotiable. Western guests have been arrested and deported for ignoring this law in more conservative countries. Each night at sunset, families and friends gather together to celebrate *iftar*, the breaking of the fast.

In general, things happen more slowly during Ramadan, with businesses operating on a reduced schedule. Shops may be open and closed at unusual times. There are often private places for non-Muslims to satisfy their hunger and thirst. Ask the Concierge at your hotel where these places are.

Greetings & Conversation Etiquette:

Learning the basic greeting is always a sign of respect in whichever country you are visiting. The usual greeting of *Salam aleikum* (Peace be upon you) is used when meeting someone in an Arab country, to which one replies: *Aleikum salam*. Refrain from any physical contact when greeting (e.g., shaking hands or kissing). Placing the palm of the right hand on the chest, bowing the head a little and closing one's eyes means "thank you" (in the name of Allah).

Enquiries about health, well-being, and the generally profuse greetings that Muslims engage in at the start of a conversation may seem to take up an inordinate amount of time to a Westerner. But to an Arab it is an important part of establishing friendly relations. It is considered improper for a man to ask about another man's wife or any female member of his family.

Conversation Taboos:

- Purdah requires women to avoid men who are not their husbands or family members and to cover most of their bodies. Purdah applies between members of the opposite sex who are not married (*mahram*). Males may not enquire about another male's wife or female family members in conversation as it is a sign of disrespect. Likewise, a woman may be charged with prostitution for socializing with a man who is not a relative or husband.

- Steer clear of discussing anything of a religious nature, particularly if your views are critical of Islam and of Muslims. Avoid getting into any political debates, especially regarding Israel and the United States. Do not broach any subject on male/female relations or anything of a sexual nature.

Behavior in Mosques:

A mosque is a place of worship for followers of Islam. Mosques are also considered to be shelters for the homeless. It is important that one's dress and behavior in a mosque be dictated to by modesty, respect and reverence at all times. - Read more about appropriate dress in the Dressing Etiquette section in this chapter.

Removing your shoes prior to entering a mosque is a sign of respect. There is a special carpet provided at the entrance for this purpose. Most mosques have an attendant at the entrance who can help you with the appropriate behavior if you're unsure of what to do, and even supply you with a cover up if needed. Never remove your shoes while standing on the stone walkway as this means that you are bringing dirt into a sacred space, which will earn you a stern lecture from the attendant.

Do not walk directly in front of people praying, or speak during prayers or lectures. Wait at the rear of the mosque until prayers have finished before walking in. Never take pictures of people in mosques, particularly the women.

Appropriate Social Behavior:

The Middle Eastern Islamic culture is patriarchal and hierarchal. Males are the head of the family, with the father having the last word. It is unacceptable for a man to gaze at, or touch, a woman who is not their wife or direct relative. Men and women are not allowed to mix in close quarters unless they are family members.

If a Middle Eastern male has to address a strange woman, he more than likely will let his gaze rest on a patch of wall just above her head, or on the floor, and address her in the third person. In the Middle East, women never travel or book a hotel on their own. Many hotels in Saudi Arabia will not give a couple a room without sighting their marriage license first.

Middle Eastern custom condones the outward display of affection between male friends, but never between members of the opposite sex. Men will give their male friends long handshakes, grasp elbows, walk hand-in-hand and hug. However, public displays of affection between men and women in the Muslim world are not only considered offensive, but forbidden. Refrain from kissing, caressing, or even holding your partner or husband's hand while traveling in the Middle East until you've reached the privacy of your room.

Although eye contact between husband and wife, or direct relatives, is acceptable during conversation in a private home, it becomes unacceptable in public or when the eye contact is prolonged between people who are not married or related. If you are a Western woman traveling in the Middle East and you don't want to make eye contact with a stranger unwittingly when out in public, the use of dark glasses is a useful tool.

It is often customary for people to remove their shoes at the entrance of someone's home before entering as a sign of respect. Oversize slippers are sometimes provided for you to put on.

When visiting someone's home, the men's group will more than likely be separate to the women's group, even eating at separate times. When sitting in the company of Arabs, take care to sit with your feet firmly planted on the ground. Avoid stretching your legs out, showing the soles of your feet, sitting with the left hand behind your back, or crossing your legs. Also avoid sitting up higher than others, leaning against walls, slouching in chairs, putting feet on the furniture, and keeping hands in your pockets. These are all signs of disrespect.

The issue of personal space may be much closer in Arab countries than in the West or Europe, so don't back away when the person of the same sex that you are speaking with steps forward.

It is considered rude. However, it is forbidden for a man to stand close, stare at or touch a woman.

Special respect is paid to older people in the Middle East. Always stand when an older person enters a room, greet the eldest people in a room before others present, stand when speaking to an elderly person, and serve older people first at a meal table.

In the West, we tend to have a preoccupation with time and the need to fit as much as we can into an allocated slot. The Middle East, however, has a more relaxed mentality towards punctuality. Being late is not a sign of disrespect and does not warrant an apology, unless the tardiness is excessive (more than 90 minutes). Refrain from looking at your watch or clock, or appearing to be in a hurry, during a get-together with Arab hosts. Doing so suggests that you consider your host unworthy of your time.

There seems to be a growing trend in Arab countries, particularly in Qatar, for women to smoke the *hookah* (water pipe). However, despite the chain-smoking taxi drivers, smoke-filled coffee shops, or the gurgling of the ubiquitous *hookahs,* a large majority of Middle Eastern men still find the sight of a woman smoking distasteful and unacceptable. If you feel the need to smoke it would be best to do so in private surroundings.

Muslims forbid the drinking of alcohol, although it may be served to foreigners and non-Muslims in international bars or hotels. As an extra precaution for women, it is best to abstain from drinking alcohol in public.

While rude hand gestures, like "giving the finger," cause hostility in most countries, the one-finger salute can land you in jail in a conservative Muslim country. Pointing your finger, or even a pen, at someone while speaking is considered a threat in the Arab world so avoid doing this at all costs. In Iran, even the "thumbs up" gesture is considered rude.

Gift Giving Etiquette:

Nomadic cultures in the Middle East have a tradition of hospitality to travelers, and to give a gift to your host is a symbol of respect and appreciation for their hospitality. Your host will more than likely give their gift offering to you first and it will more often than not be of a high standard of workmanship and value. To reciprocate, make sure that your gift is of similar good quality.

Gifts are presented using the right hand or both hands. The left hand is never to be used alone when handing someone a gift as it is considered unclean.

When dining in someone's home, it is customary to bring flowers or pastries. The proper way to give a gift is to apologize for its inadequacy, which gives the recipient the cue to fuss over it all the more. Gifts must always be elegantly wrapped, even though they may not be opened when received but placed on a table and not mentioned.

Gifts or food products that are forbidden by the *Qur'an* are those made from "scavengers," pork, birds, and shellfish. Any leather items made from pig skin or ostrich skin cannot be given as a gift, nor any food from these groups. Avoid giving gifts made with shell/Mother of Pearl.

In the Muslim culture, the *Qur'an* also forbids alcohol. Gifts of liquor or any product that contains alcohol, such as perfume, should never be selected as a gift. Artwork that consists of sculptures, drawings or photos depicting the human body, particularly a nude or partially nude female body, is definitely not an acceptable gift.

An ideal gift for a devout Muslim is a compass as, each day, they must face Mecca for prayers. No matter where in the world they happen to be, they can easily find the correct direction to Mecca with a compass. Other suitable gifts include anything made of silver, cashmere, porcelain, crystal and precious stones.

It is considered disrespectful for a male to present a gift to an Arab colleague's wife. Likewise, a woman must never present a gift to an Arab male who is not her husband, father, or brother.

The Custom of Taarof:

A common custom in the Middle Eastern Arab nations is *Taarof*, a traditional practice that is meant to provide dignity, respect, and honor for both the guest and the host.

Translating to "offering," it is a system of politeness that includes protests to compliments, the belittling of one's own accomplishments, and other verbal and non-verbal communications of humility. In adherence to *taarof*, it is common for a person to decline an offer of food and beverages on the first, even second, offer. Instead, the offer is taken up when the insistence becomes greater.

Dining Etiquette:

"If a pot is cooking, the friendship will stay warm."

– ARAB PROVERB.

The Middle Eastern tradition of hospitality and generosity towards visitors goes back to the culture of the desert, when hospitality enabled inhabitants of the Arabian Peninsula to survive thirst, hunger, and sudden raids. An invitation to visit someone's home, whether just to have coffee and figs or to join the family in a meal, is an honor that must never be turned down.

In the more conservative homes, the men's group will more than likely be separate to the women's group, even eating at separate times. Food that is designated as permissible according to Islamic law is called halal. The opposite of this word is *haraam*.

Although the more sophisticated households and restaurants in the Arab world may dine Continental style (knife and fork), the majority of the Arab population take their food from a common plate in the center of the table, where people scoop up *hummus* (a Levantine Arab dip made from chickpeas) and other foodstuff with pita bread. Always remember that eating and passing food must always be done with the right hand, as the left hand is generally regarded as unclean.

Middle Easterners consider it impolite to eat everything on one's plate. Leaving food becomes a symbol of abundance and serves to compliment the host.

When inviting an Arab friend out for a meal, always select a restaurant that serves halal food. Never have alcohol served.

Dressing Etiquette:

In Islam, a woman's clothing must not attract unnecessary attention, nor any part of her body be seen. Although the appropriate dress code for Arab nations may pose a bit of a dilemma for most foreign guests, it would be unwise to overlook this issue, as the way a woman dresses in the Arab world will influence how the locals view and treat her.

There are many interpretations of appropriate dress for women in the Middle East, depending on the conservativeness of each society. The factors that decide how conservative a nation is depends on its degree of patriarchy (role of the male as the main authority figure), how religious the people are, and the roles that women play in that particular society. Because ongoing volatility in politics continuously changes the accepted mode of behavior for women in the Middle East, it's important to keep updated on any new developments from government websites before you travel.

The key to culturally correct dress for women in the Arab world is to work out what the local women are wearing and follow them. To start with, take along some long skirts and dresses (mid-shin) and loose blouses or shirts with three-quarter or long sleeves. The blouse must be left untucked and long enough to cover the hips and your backside. Keep the colors of your clothes fairly muted and discreet (not bright or showy) so as not to draw attention to yourself. Do not forget to cover your head with a scarf or veil.

Once you have established what the local women wear in a specific area, find out where they shop. Have a look at the range of women's clothing that can be purchased in the shopping malls, souks, or even large supermarkets of your host country. In some nations, the variety of colors and prints in long cotton robes and coats have become wider and more fashionable over the years. Wear these robes on your visit as they will be far more comfortable in the heat and you will be much better received by the locals.

Iranian women dress with a great sense of style, wearing a long coat in fashionable colors over their regular clothes and a scarf covering their heads. The colors can range from muted greens and duck egg blues, subtle beiges, and rustic reds, with decorative buttons adding an ornamental finish. The coats must not be fitted and must be long enough to reach mid-shin. Legs or ankles must not be bared, with women wearing socks and thick hose to cover the flesh, although this rule has relaxed a little over the past few years. Underneath their coats, the women can wear what they like.

Keep in mind that although rural women that work the fields may wear less restrictive garments, lighter in color and weight, than they do in the cities, their values tend to be more conservative.

At the risk of stating the obvious, shorts, even if they are knee length, skimpy skirts, and tight fitting/low cut clothes, are all highly inappropriate in a Muslim country.

To be on the safe side, leave your nails unvarnished when visiting any Arab nation, at least until you have established the lay of the land. In some countries, foreign women are sometimes handed a petrol-soaked rag to wipe clean their varnished nails at the airport. Varnished nails are considered pollution of the body and any woman with varnished nails is seen as unfit to pray.

Always check the rules for women swimming when visiting any beaches in the Arab world, or before making use of the hotel swimming pool. In Tehran's Revolution Hotel, for example, only men are allowed to swim in public. If women are allowed to swim, consider the type of bathing suit that you will wear. A full piece, with a modest cover-up when out of the water, would be more appropriate. It's best to leave the bikini at home.

To wear or not to wear hijab:

Hijab refers to any woman's dress that follows Islamic principles. Muslim women are free to choose whether to wear veils and scarves in some Arab nations like Lebanon, Syria and Egypt.

The wearing of the *niqab* (veil worn by women that completely covers the face) and the *burka* (face mask made of leather or stiff fabric which covers the entire face except for the eyes) are more cultural choices of specific nations rather than the literal translation of the *Qur'an*. However, liberal Muslim women and even non-Muslim women wear veils out of fear of mistreatment by religious fanatics in the more conservative nations. It is important to note that this fanaticism is by no means a true reflection of Islam, or of all Muslims. Again, it is always best to check government websites for political updates prior to travel in the Middle East.

Listed below are the various modes of appropriate dress for women in the Middle East:

Abaya – Generally worn in Persian Gulf countries, the *abaya* is a black cloak with arm slits that falls from the top of the head to the ankles.

Burka – The *burka* is a face mask made of leather or stiff fabric which covers the entire face, except for the eyes. This is usually worn by women in the Gulf countries.

Chador – Worn by women in Iran and by Lebanese *Shi'ites,* the chador is a square of fabric that falls from the top of the head to the ankles and is pinned closed under the chin.

Hijab – Literally meaning a "curtain," *hijab* refers to any woman's dress that follows Islamic principles.

Magneh – The *magneh* is a cowl-like head covering that is worn by the women in Iran.

Niqab – The niqab is a veil worn by women that completely covers the face.

Roosarie – An Iranian name for a head scarf.

Salwar Kameez – Worn by women in Pakistan, the *salwar kameez* is a silky calf-length tunic worn over pants, with shawls of matching fabric tossed loosely over the head.

Shayla – An Arabic word for head scarf.

Safety Precautions:

Women in Western dress may be vulnerable to physical and verbal harassment in this part of the world, particularly in crowded areas. Exercise caution, dress modestly, and travel in the company of a male friend, colleague, husband, or partner whenever possible.

Wearing a fake wedding ring, even if you are not married, means that you are connected to a man, which commands more respect in the Arab world. If you happen to be traveling with a man, you may want to say that he is your husband in order to avoid any extra attention.

Avoid walking alone after dark in isolated places. Avoid sitting in the front seat of the taxis as this signals availability and you may leave yourself open to assault or molestation. On public transport, always sit next to women if possible.

Avoid eating alone in restaurants and cafés if possible. If you are eating out with another woman, sit in the family section in restaurants and cafés. You will have a better chance of avoiding stares and unwanted attention. If you need directions, it is best to ask women. If you feel that you are being followed by a man and you feel that your safety could be threatened, duck into a shop, fuel station, or hotel lobby.

Never disclose personal information that may cause your Arab host or colleague discomfort, or to judge you harshly (e.g., issues such as single motherhood, homosexuality, and/or divorce). Even though these issues may be widely discussed and accepted in your own culture, remember that the Arab world has different values to the West.

It's a good idea to wear dark glasses when out in public. Not only are they good for eye protection from the dust and glare, they also stop you from accidentally meeting men's eyes, an action that can be interpreted as flirtation in more conservative countries.

Avoid responding to lewd comments, cat calls, or remarks made by younger men, as they are only looking for a reaction. It is best to ignore them and just keep walking.

fourteen

Russia

"Neither man or nation can exist without a sublime idea."

– FYODOR DOSTOYEVSKY, RUSSIAN NOVELIST AND WRITER.

Historic Influences:

Russia is a huge country with a population of about 143,420,300 (estimate for 2010), making it also one of the world's most populous nations. Comprised of more than 100 nationalities, the Russians, a Slavic people, comprise more than 80 per cent of the total population.

Much had been said about the Russian soul. It's been described as sensitive, imaginative, compassionate, poetic, mystical, and fatalistic, with an inclination to tears. Several factors have conspired to create such a national character, the first of which is living for centuries under extremely harsh climatic conditions. With its land more than 400 kilometers (248.50 miles) away from the sea, immense mountain ranges block the moderate temperatures that blow in from the Indian and Pacific oceans. European Russia and Siberia endure the harshest climates of all as they lack any topographic conditions that can add protection from the harsh icy winds that sweep in from the Arctic and North Atlantic oceans.

This factor has molded the Russians' strength and ability to endure extreme hardship.

Russia has also had a long history of totalitarianism, which has resulted in their rather fatalistic approach to living. The desire to work individually under personal initiative was suppressed by the Czarist and Communist states.

The ability to withstand harsh climatic conditions, plus their ability to endure brutal totalitarian regimes, have given the Russians their communal spirit and belief in working jointly for the common good. While the Soviet/Communist value system has eroded through the years, the process of adapting to the Western value system of individualism has been a gradual one.

Traits of the Russian Character:

On the surface, Russians may seem cold and distant. Underneath, however, you will find a highly sentimental, and sometimes melancholic, side to them once you have earned their trust. They have a high tolerance level for hardship and injustice, which makes them understanding by nature, forgive willingly, and believe in second chances. But when a Russian's temper explodes, which would more than likely be because you have betrayed their trust, they are a force to be reckoned with.

For Russians, too much order is not good. They have a dislike for rules and distrust authority. They have the belief that all laws are there to be manipulated. When something is not allowed in Russia but someone really wants it, then it is usually permitted as an exception.

Russian laziness has an almost dreamy and meditative quality to it, thinking over and over if something is worth lifting a finger for. However, when they are engaged and emotionally involved in the task at hand, they can beat all records in efficiency.

Greeting & Conversation Etiquette:

If you expect warmth and all smiles when meeting a Russian for the first time, you will be disappointed. Russians tend to have a naturally suspicious nature and will be rather cool and cautious when they meet people for the first time. You might even find them speaking metaphorically or cryptically. But when a Russian starts standing closer when speaking with you, touching your arm, giving you hugs, backslaps and kisses on the cheeks, you know you've made a friend. And once you've gained their trust and friendship, as far as they're concerned it is a friendship for life. However, once you've made an undertaking with your Russian friend, follow up on your promise as they will hold you to it.

While public displays of affection in Russia are OK, speaking loudly and gesticulating wildly are not. Russians prefer a moderate tone of voice when conversing and never gesticulate excessively. In fact, they have little trust for people that are loud, viewing them as uneducated or suspicious.

A Russian can be frank to the point of bluntness, as they value honesty over the niceties. So be "real" instead of "nice" with a Russian, as it will be much more appreciated. They also tend to take such greetings as "Hi! How are you?" quite literally. If you greet a Russian in this manner, don't be surprised to hear them expounding on their health.

Russians are extremely educated, so be prepared for them to discuss the history or culture of your own country. You may also be subjected to personal inquiries, and it is up to you how much you are willing to respond to the questioning, as it may even get a tad intrusive. But when the shoe is on the other foot, Russians don't appreciate being asked questions of a personal nature.

There is tremendous affection for children in the Russian culture, so if you're stuck for something to talk about, you may want to pull out the photographs of your children or ask them about theirs. It works every time.

Russians are extremely educated, so be prepared for them to discuss the history or culture of your own country. You may also be subjected to personal inquiries, and it is up to you how much you are willing to respond to the questioning, as it may even get a tad intrusive. But when the shoe is on the other foot, Russians don't appreciate being asked questions of a personal nature.

There is tremendous affection for children in the Russian culture, so if you're stuck for something to talk about, you may want to pull out the photographs of your children or ask them about theirs. It works every time.

Basic Greetings:

Russians are delighted if you make the effort to speak even a few sentences of their language. However, if your Russian friends speak English, your determination to speak Russian may cause them to think that their English is not good enough, so sound them out first.

Here are some helpful Russian phrases, which are written the way that they are pronounced:

Dobraye ootro	Good morning
Dobriy den	Good afternoon
Dobriy vyecher	Good evening
Zdrastvooyte	Hello
Preevyet	Hi

Kak pazhivayesh?	How are you?
Spaseeba preekrasna!	Fine, thanks
Neeploha!	Not so bad
Kak vas zavoot?	What is your name?
Meenya zavoot...	My name is ....
Spaseeba	Thank you
Bal'shoye spaseeba	Thank you very much
Pazhalooysta	You're welcome
Eezveeneete	Sorry
Prasteete	Excuse me
Da sveedaneeya	Goodbye

Conversation Taboos:

Russians are enthusiastic about politics and the challenge of living in Russia. However, openly criticizing their culture or country is a bad idea, as the Russian national pride runs deep.

Appropriate Social Behavior:

"One can know a man from his laugh, and if you like a man's laugh before you know anything of him, you may confidently say that he is a good man."

– FYODOR DOSTOYEVSKY, RUSSIAN NOVELIST AND WRITER.

Most Russians do not have houses. They either rent or own apartments that are at least 30 years old. It is still common for newlyweds to live with one of the parents, or for the parents to divide up a house or apartment so that two families can live there. In a nutshell, space is at a premium, so the social etiquette when visiting someone's home in Russia will be different to that in most Anglo-Saxon cultures.

Always remove your coat upon entering any home or building. Most Russian homes and buildings have a coatroom. At the entryway of your host's home, remove your shoes. In general, Russians do not wear their shoes inside the house. Often your hosts will have a set of slippers for you to wear during your visit.

Unlike most Anglo-Saxon cultures, Russians will not give you a tour of their home, so avoid putting them on the spot by asking them to show you around. Resist the temptation of being nosy and peeking into the bedrooms as this will not be appreciated.

Upon entering someone's home in Russia, you might want to keep a lid on those compliments. Russians are extremely generous, to the point where they will literally give you the shirts off their own backs if you compliment them on it. Seriously, if you begin complimenting an object in their home too effusively, your hosts may insist that you take it with you. However, they will expect the same treatment when they visit your home in return.

When seated in Russian company, do not cross your legs with the ankle on the knee, as it's impolite to show people the soles of your shoes. The soles of the feet are considered unclean, and to show the soles constitutes a lack of respect. Needless to say, never put your feet on the furniture.

Certain peculiarities of the Russian character may seem weird to the Western mind. For example, Russians find constant smiling false and irritating. Russians smile only if they have a good reason, and find the Western habit of smiling just because one feels good annoying.

As a foreigner, you'll be expected to be punctual for all your appointments. However, expect to be kept waiting when you arrive for an appointment in Russia, have your appointment cancelled unexpectedly, or have your schedule changed several times. Do not expect an apology either. The Russians are known for their great patience, and this is often used as a ploy to test yours.

Elderly women are respected in Russia, and it is considered polite to offer them seats in the Metro, and to defer to them in social engagements.

Russian Superstitions:

Superstitions are taken seriously in Russia, so it's best to pay heed to them:

- Never shake hands through an open door, or you are bound to quarrel.

- Don't sit at the corner of a dinner table, or you will not stay married for longer than seven years.

- If you must return to a home or room to retrieve something that you have left behind, make sure you look in the mirror before leaving that room again.

- If a fork falls, a woman is going to come into the room or into your life; if a knife falls, then a man will appear.

Gift Giving Etiquette:

Bringing a gift to someone's home is universally accepted, and nowhere more than in Russia. A traditional craft from your country will always be appreciated by your Russian host.

A gift of chocolates, dessert or pastries, or good wine, is always appreciated if you have been invited to someone's home for dinner, while an expensive perfume or cologne is an acceptable "thank you" for an overnight stay. Russians spend a lot of money on gifts, so don't be cheap with your gifts.

Your host will almost always open your present straight away, and you'll know if your host genuinely likes their gift if they are effusive in their praise.

Flowers are given almost exclusively for women, so bring along a bunch for a wife, sister, or mother of your host. Make sure that you bring an odd number, as even numbers are for funerals. The colors pink, cream-colored, orange and blue are acceptable. Avoid giving yellow or white flowers, which are used for funerals, and red flowers, which are considered a romantic gift.

Russians love their children; it's a good idea to bring any children a small gift such as a toy or candy. However, giving a pregnant woman a gift before the baby is born is considered bad luck.

Dining Etiquette:

You may want to forget about your dieting when dining in a Russian home as your hosts will feed you until you are at bursting point. And since the Russians are great "sitters," make use of the restroom prior to being seated for your meal, as it's not polite to get up until you are invited to leave the table. In most cases, that could be a couple of hours or more from the moment that you sit down. Add to the equation copious amounts of vodka, and I guarantee you'll be squirming in your seat halfway through your meal.

Russians dine in the Continental style, which means that the fork is held in the left hand and the knife in the right while eating. It's considered rude to begin eating until your host invites you to start. If you are the guest of honor, you will be served first. Like standard European etiquette, it is rude to rest your elbows on the table, although your hands should be visible

The foundations of Russian cuisine is largely based on rural cooking in an often harsh climate. Soups and stews with meat and fish are flavorsome and characterized by a wonderful array of sauces and gravies. It is acceptable to use the bread to mop up the wonderful juices. But leave a small amount of food on your plate, as this indicates that your host has provided ample hospitality.

Remember to say, "Thank you, everything was very tasty" to the one who made the dish before you leave the table. "Very tasty" in Russian sounds something like *oh-chen koos-nah.*

In restaurants, Russians will not hesitate to join a table with strangers rather than dine alone. Counting expenses or checking the bill when the meal is over will seem petty to a Russian as it is natural that everyone contributes to the "common good" as much as one can.

Drinking Etiquette:

In Russia, there will be toasts. Endless toasts. With vodka. Straight. This must be downed in one shot, never sipped. Here are some steps that will ensure that you come out of your Russian drinking experience with your head, stomach and liver intact:

- Wait for your host or hostess to begin the round of toasts. To drink your vodka before the first toast has been made is considered bad form.

- Keep your glass raised throughout the toast, then clink glasses with the others in your group before downing the shot of vodka. Russians never mix their vodka with juices or soda. To do so would be sacrilegious. Vodka is drunk straight as a shot, which means downing the entire glass in one swallow.

- You must offer a second toast to your host or hostess, thanking them for their gracious hospitality, and sending greetings from all your family and friends back home. Failing to do so would be impolite.

- It's a good idea to propose a toast to your hosts early in the evening while you're still coherent. Putting it off for later will only force you to drink more than you should.

- Another round of toasting follows after dinner, and not participating in it is an affront to polite Russian etiquette.

- Take bites of food in between your vodka shots. Not only does it help absorb the alcohol, it is also good form.

- Pace yourself after the first round of drinks. After the tenth round, you will finally understand why.

- The phrase *Choot-Choot* will be your salvation from getting totally plastered on vodka in Russia. *Choot-Choot* means "so-so," This tells the person doing the pouring that, although you're a good sport and would love to match the group shot for shot, you're unable to keep up with a full glass every time.

Dressing Etiquette:

Pardon the pun, but the Russian winter is nothing to sneeze at, particularly St. Petersburg which is significantly colder than Moscow. During the winter months, St. Petersburg can be in the dark for 23 hours of the day. Despite the brutal cold, however, all buildings are centrally heated, with the heating turned on in October and not turned off until April. The key to dressing appropriately in Russia, therefore, is to dress in layers that you can peel off as soon as you get indoors.

Staples for the Russian winter include a very warm coat, a lined hat that covers your ears, thick woolen scarves, well-insulated gloves, and lined boots. A long coat is better than a parka for those harsh Russian winters as you will need the extra length to protect your lower back and legs from the chill. Although not ethically or politically correct (try telling that to the Russians), fur has always been the outer wear of choice in Russia as nothing else comes close to it for warmth. However, may I recommend some wonderful alternatives to fur like a good quality down coat, which you can press down to fit into your suitcase and wear with confidence when you return to your own country.

You can never have enough scarves in Russia, so bring plenty of these with you. An even better idea is to buy some when you get there. The Russians are a fashion conscious lot, and they do love their scarves, so you'll find an exciting selection in the stores.

Women in business dress conservatively in Russia, preferring dresses and skirt-suits to pants. Keep your dress colors dark or muted. Dressing for a dinner at someone's home is a more relaxed affair, so trousers and a nice blouse or sweater with a jacket is fine. Jeans are fine for sightseeing during the day, but remember to cover your head when visiting a Russian Orthodox church.

As all buildings are centrally heated in Russia, you will always find a *gardarov* on the ground floor, where you will be required to check in your coat in exchange for a number. Coats are considered street wear in Russia and it's bad form to wear them indoors. Remember to remove anything of value from your pockets when checking in your coat (e.g.. cell phone, passport, money). You can retrieve your coat from the coat room attendant when you exit the building. The standard tip is 10 or 20 rubles.

For those of you ladies that are interested in visiting a Russian nightclub, you'll need to get past the doorman first, who has the power to veto who gets in and who doesn't. This means you'll need to be under 30 years of age, drop dead gorgeous, and dress like a street walker. Secondly, you'll need plenty of money as they are incredibly expensive.

Safety Precautions:

Many Russians still have the notion that all foreigners are rich, so tourist scams are, unfortunately, common. Some may argue that the wealth is there to be shared. However, it is for this reason that tourists should be especially vigilant with their personal belongings around tourist attractions, such as Red Square and the Metro.

There is a scam in Russia that involves dropping money on the ground for a passer-by to pick up. The passer-by picks up the money and returns it to the person that dropped it, only to be told that it is not the correct amount. Be on the alert, do not pick up any money from the ground, and never get involved with any disputes in a public place. Just keep walking on.

Only exchange foreign currency directly with bank tellers, never with anyone from the streets or a stranger in the bank queue. Credit card and ATM frauds are also common. Always keep your credit card in sight during the transactions, and withdraw money from secure ATM sites in shopping centers and department stores.

Never leave food unattended, or accept food and beverages from strangers. Drinks and food are frequently "spiked" at bars and nightclubs.

fifteen

Scandinavia

"Dignity is like a perfume; those who use it are scarcely
conscious of it."

– QUEEN CHRISTINA OF SWEDEN

Historic Influences:

While evidence of human settlement in Scandinavia dates back
10,000 years ago, with a sophisticated lifestyle revolving around
hunting, fishing, and agrarianism, it is the barbaric Vikings and
their seafaring adventurousness that remain synonymous with
Scandinavian history. A modestly literate people, not much is
known about their 200-year reign of terror (c. 850AD–1050AD)
save for the accounts of their victims from England, Scotland,
Ireland, France and Germany. Written accounts of Scandinavia's
history start to make an appearance with the introduction of
Christianity during the Middle Ages, with Denmark embracing
Catholicism first in about 829 AD.

Northern Europe has been the cultural, historical, and political
playground of Norway, Sweden, Denmark and Finland through
the ages, with the Swedish settling, hunting, and trading in
Finland for centuries. After the Swedish revolt in 1521, however,

loyalties between the historical monarchies became divided, with the Norwegians and Danish on one side, and Swedish and Finns in the other. Traces of these alliances still remain in their languages, with similarities between the Danish, Norwegian, and Swedish languages. Finnish is its own language, with some similarities to Estonian.

Most non-Scandinavians still tend to lump the Danes, Finns, and Swedes in the same group. However, differences do exist, as does a long-standing sibling rivalry between Sweden and Denmark. On the whole, the Swedes tend to be more organized, structured, and systematic, while the Danes tend to be more impulsive, striving towards greater expression of the individual. And just like one big happy family, the Swedes tell jokes about the Norwegians, the Norwegians about the Finns, and the Danes about the Swedes. They will appreciate you all the more if you take the time to understand their subtle differences.

Greeting & Conversation Etiquette:

The proper Swedish greeting is to offer your hand and say *god dag,* while maintaining good eye contact. This literally means "good day." Most of the time, a simple *hej* will suffice, even if you do not know the person. Do not be surprised if a complete stranger smiles at you and greets you with *hej.* It is expected of you to respond in the same way. When leaving, Swedes say *hej då.*

Once a social rapport has been established, you may find that the handshake will be replaced with a European-style air kiss on both cheeks. To be on the safe side, allow your Swedish contact to set the pace.

In Sweden, one hears *tack* ("thank you") much more often than in other countries. Swedes thank when they take and when they give. A clerk in the bank can welcome you by a "*ja, tack*" meaning "How can I help you?"

Swedes say "*du*" (the pronoun "you") to each other, and expect to address a person by his or her first name. Titles are not important in Sweden, even in business. So instead of saying, "Good morning director Andersson", the Swedes simply say "Good morning Inga". However, it's best for foreigners to err on the side of caution at first by using *Herr* (Mr) or *Fru* (Mrs), followed by your counterpart's last name. They will appreciate the initial respect shown to them, and will quickly set you straight as to the preferred way they'd like to be addressed.

The exceptions are Their Majesties and the Crown Princess, whom you would address in the third person, (i.e., "His Majesty" or "The Crown Princess"). Similarly, older, upper-class Swedes can be more formal, avoiding the pronoun "you." Instead, they refer to people in the third person. When speaking with Mrs Andersson, they may say, "How is Mrs Andersson feeling today?" When spoken to in the third person, one must respond in the same manner.

The Swedish people value their personal space, so maintain a distance of two arm-lengths between you and the person with whom you are conversing. For similar reasons, do not backslap, embrace, touch a Swede unless you know them very well, or gesticulate wildly when speaking. The Swedish keep their body language and hand gestures to a minimum.

Avoid having your hands in your pockets when conversing with someone as it can be seen as a sign of arrogance. Similarly, avoid gum chewing, slouching, or leaning against things.

Swedish people also use fewer words to express themselves and are rather direct when they communicate. They do not appreciate an overly flowery manner of speech and find the use of sarcasm and irony unnecessary. Profanities in one's speech doesn't go down too well with the Swedes either.

The Swedes are a quiet and subdued people who do not get emotional when discussing a problem or debating an issue. Heated debates are unusual, and criticism has to be presented in a non-personal and diplomatic way. During business discussions, it is expected to remain cool and controlled. Never feel the need to fill in the pauses in your conversation with a Swede either, as they are very comfortable with silences.

Swedish people tend to keep their private lives to themselves and keep their chit-chat to general questions like "Have you had a nice weekend?" Having clear-cut boundaries between work and personal life allows them to respect each other's personal space, focus on their jobs, and avoid inefficiency in the workplace.

To a Swede, gender equality is a given. So compliments from men on the way that a lady looks or dresses, particularly if the person is not a close friend, is considered patronizing and condescending.

Whatever the topic of conversation, avoid superficiality in conversation with the Swedish, as they are good at sensing whether you know what you're talking about or not, and are likely to lose interest in you very quickly if you don't. The Swedes are not so good at small talk either except when discussing the weather and nature. They have a particularly good appreciation for nature as they see themselves as very much a part of it. Inquire about your Swedish friend's countryside home as most of them own one and are quick to leave the workplace on Friday to spend their weekends there.

Other welcome topics of conversation include Sweden's economy (only if you know what you're talking about), high standard of living, sports, architecture and history.

Conversation Taboos:

- Steer clear of any topic of a sexual nature as the Swedes consider this crass and intrusive. Similarly, Swedish people are egalitarian and humble by nature and find it difficult to abide by anyone who boasts about how much money they make or how successful they are.

- It's not seen as good form in Sweden to be critical about a person, especially when the person isn't present, even if it's about their boss or employer.

- Never criticize any aspect of the Swedish culture or praise another city in Sweden over the one you're visiting. Never compare Sweden to Finland, Norway or Denmark. Remember that sibling rivalry is alive and well between these northern European nations. The Swedes are proud of their own unique towns, regions, cultures and identities.

- Don't be offended if a Swede tells a joke about war that you might consider insensitive. The Swedes have not had a war for more than 200 years and have no point of reference to the war sufferings of other countries.

Appropriate Social Behavior:

"It is necessary to try to pass one's self always; this occupation ought to last as long as life."

– QUEEN CHRISTINA OF SWEDEN

The Swedes have a high respect for rules and punctuality, with little tolerance for cultural variation on these issues. Rules to a Swede are a sign of respect and efficiency, with the same rules applying to all, irrespective of age, gender, or status. Because of this characteristic, many people believe that the Swedish people are inflexible and unable to act freely. A Swede would argue that it is the rules that give one's mind and imagination the freedom to focus on more creative things.

The Swede's respect for rules extends to all things mundane, like waiting patiently on the curb until the light turns green at pedestrian crossings. In the absence of lights, Swedish drivers are careful and respectful, usually stopping for pedestrians.

When at bus stops, stores, sales desks and other public spaces, wait patiently for your turn, no matter how long it takes. If visiting ticket offices or shops with a personal sales service, look for the queue ticket machine, press the button, get your number, and wait until your number shows up on the display. Like in England, queue jumping is frowned upon in Sweden.

Swedish companies reflect Swedish society in that they are not hierarchical or patriarchal in structure and attitude. An executive is considered to be a specialist in managing companies, therefore not socially superior to a specialist in any other field. Status and hierarchy in the Swedish workplace is largely replaced by personal responsibility, team work, and the effective exchange of information, with problems being solved in an informal and pragmatic way.

While business colleagues may eventually become friends, many Swedes enjoy their old friendships with childhood or college companions more, and will take their time in getting to know you before they consider you a friend.

Do not think of having even one drink and driving in Sweden, The Swedish drink-driving laws are strict.. If you're caught, do not attempt to bribe the police officers either as it will only land you in bigger trouble. Sweden has one of the lowest corruption levels in the world.

Smoking is prohibited almost everywhere in Sweden. Pay attention to specially designated smoking areas equipped with windproof ashtrays. Otherwise, expect to smoke outside the building, where ashtrays are provided.

Gift Giving Etiquette:

Gifts are expected in social events in Sweden, especially when invited for dinner. Flowers, good-quality liquor, wine, cake, or good-quality chocolates, are appropriate gifts for your host or hostess. If your host has children, you may want to bring them some candy. Avoid giving your hosts crystal items or any object made in Sweden.

If you choose to bring flowers, make sure that they are wrapped beautifully, and that the bouquet is an odd number (except for the number 13), an old European tradition. Avoid chrysanthemums or white lilies, since they are used for funerals, or red roses or orchids, unless the flowers are a romantic gesture.

If you are staying with a family, an appropriate thank-you gift would be a high-quality product that represents your country (e.g., gourmet foodstuffs, coffee table books about your home country or city), or anything that reflects your host's personal tastes.

Gift giving is not common among business associates at the beginning of a business relationship, although it is appropriate to present your business colleague with a high-quality gift as you are closing your business transaction. Choose something practical rather than one that may be perceived as lavish. Books about your country, as well as desk accessories, all make appropriate gifts.

Dining Etiquette:

Although the Swedes may appear friendly and informal when you first meet them, they will still maintain some boundaries until they get to know you better. Do not be offended that you are not invited to your Swedish colleague or friend's home straight away, as the Swedes will take their time before the relationship gets to this level. But there is also another reason at play here; it is not common in Sweden to have housekeepers or hired help for the home or the children. Dinner guests would only add to their already considerable domestic load. However, in late spring or summer, you may be invited to your host's countryside house. If that is the case, then leisure clothes and easy conversation become the order of the day.

Punctuality is important in all business and social gatherings in Sweden. This means that when you are invited for dinner at eight, show up at eight on the dot. It is important to let your hosts know as soon as possible if you have been delayed and the reason why. And it better be a valid reason or you lose all credibility.

When attending a dinner party, wait to be told where to sit as there may be a seating plan. As in Britain, table manners are Continental, which means holding the fork in the left hand and the knife in the right. Always keep your hands visible when eating and keep your wrists resting on the edge of the table.

If you are offered second helpings, it's fine for you to refuse without offending your host. However, try a little of everything. You will be expected to finish everything on your plate as Swedes do not like wasting food. When you have finished eating, place your knife and fork across your plate with the tines facing up and the handles turned slightly to the right.

The meal at a Swedish dinner ends with the male guest of honor tapping his glass with a knife or spoon and thanking the hostess on behalf of all the guests. The female guest of honor should also thank the host.

Ring your host the following day to thank them for a lovely evening and the beautiful meal. When meeting them again after you have been a guest at their home, make it a point to thank them again. To the Swedes, you can never go wrong with an extra thank you.

Drinking Etiquette:

When at a dinner party in Sweden, it is customary to wait until your host has given a toast before you can start drinking. When toasting, make eye contact and nod to the others present before putting down your glass. The men wait for the women to put down their glasses before putting down theirs, so if you're a woman, don't wait too long to set down your glass. You'll annoy the blazes out of everyone else if you don't.

Regarding the purchase of alcohol, the Swedish government has a monopoly on its importation. This means that alcohol can only be bought from a non-profit, government-run liquor store chain named *Systembolaget*. Although the stores have a huge assortment of reasonably priced, good-quality wines from all over the world, with staff able to help with your selection, there is not a *Systembolaget* on every street corner, nor is it open on Sundays. Therefore, do plan your alcohol purchase in advance. Lighter alcoholic beverages are sold in ordinary grocery stores, and all restaurants and bars have a license to sell and serve alcohol.

Dressing Etiquette:

The Swedes are a stylish lot and wear fashionable, good quality clothing with a casual edge. Scruffy jeans and runners, or a track suit, will not quite cut it in Stockholm. The Swedes are, and expect you to be, well dressed and neatly groomed in public at all times.

Safety Precautions:

Sweden would have to be one of the safest countries in the world. Although crime is low, pick-pocketing and purse snatching are common on the streets, particularly during the warmer months (May–September). Pick-pocketing can also occur at popular tourist attractions, museums, railway stations, restaurants and other public places including hotel foyers and breakfast rooms.

Sweden experiences extremely cold winters and heavy snowfall. This may cause delays to public transport. Rockslides, floods and windstorms may also occur.

sixteen

South Africa

" If there are dreams about a beautiful South Africa, there are also roads that lead to their goal. Two of these roads could be named Goodness and Forgiveness."

– NELSON MANDELA, SOUTH AFRICAN STATESMAN, FIRST DEMOCRATICALLY ELECTED STATE PRESIDENT OF SOUTH AFRICA, AND 1993 NOBEL PRIZE WINNER FOR PEACE.

Historic Influences:

There is no single culture of South Africa. Referred to as the "Rainbow Nation," South Africa's 50-million strong population is a huge melting pot that is one of the most complex and diverse in the world. Of the 50 million South Africans scattered all over a vast rural and urban landscape, nearly 31 million are Black, 5 million are White, 3 million are Colored, and one million are Indian.

Bearing this diversity in mind, it is best to make use of the rules and guidelines of that particular culture the way that you would if you were traveling to that part of the world. For example, a number of countries in Africa have traditions based in Islam. Guidelines regarding etiquette for Muslim Nations of the Middle

East, therefore, would become applicable. The same concept would apply to the Indian and Chinese South Africans.

The South African Black majority have a substantial number of rural inhabitants who lead largely impoverished lives. However, it is among these people where you will find the strongest traditional cultural heritage. The Black population is divided into four major ethnic groups, namely Nguni, Sotho, Shangaan-Tsonga and Venda. This contrasts with the rising middle-class Black communities in the cities, who combine their roots with the internationalism of an urban environment. Urban Blacks usually speak English or Afrikaans in addition to their native tongue.

The majority of the White population is of Afrikaans descent (60%), with many of the remaining 40% being of British descent. The Afrikaner population is concentrated in the Gauteng and Free State provinces and the English population in the Western and Eastern Cape and KwaZulu Natal. Most of the Colored population live in the Northern and Western Cape provinces, while most of the Indian population lives in KwaZulu Natal.

The vast majority of Whites that live in rural areas of South Africa are Afrikaans speaking. Being of the land, their values tend to lean on the conservative and traditional side. The people from Johannesburg have a more urbane outlook on life, placing value on success and looking down on their less sophisticated rural cousins. In Cape Town, family ties, social standing, and long-term friendships are more important.

Greeting & Conversation Etiquette:

Personal relationships are important to South Africans, and their communication style will depend on their closeness to you. The more intimate people are, the more open, honest, and candid the communication. It's not unusual for a South African to slap you on the back, shake hands, or even hold hands as a sign of friendship when the relationship becomes well-established. But like all new friendships, initial tact and diplomacy are required.

The handshake, along with direct eye contact and a smile, is the most common greeting among business colleagues or people meeting for the first time. Some women do not shake hands, but merely nod their head, so it is best for men to wait for a woman to extend her hand first. It is acceptable for men to kiss a woman on the cheek if they know her well, in place of a handshake.

Like the English, the South Africans respect one another's personal space so avoid standing too close when speaking, or touching them on the arm or shoulder. As is the practice in most Western countries, keep your arms loosely by your side when engaging in conversation with someone. Speaking with your hands in your pockets, or crossed in front, implies familiarity and a lack of respect. Making frequent eye contact with the speaker and nodding in agreement shows that you are engaged and interested.

South Africans on the whole are very open with their thoughts and their feelings. When conversing, they can be direct and emphatic so avoid interrupting someone while they are in mid flow. Spend time listening to the way the locals construct their sentences. What you may perceive as funny in your country, or an acceptable turn of phrase, may not necessarily be understood in South Africa.

Similarly to Australians and the English, the South Africans love their sport, with the most popular sports being rugby, football, and cricket. Provided you know what you're talking about, conversing on these topics will endear you easily to the South Africans in any social situation. Other good topics of conversation include food, South African wines, and international travel.

Conversation Taboos:

- Due to the fact that there are so many subsets within the South African culture, the various conversation taboos will largely depend on the social sphere that you find yourself in. Many sections within South African society are fully integrated, while others still hold on to a strong colonial mentality. It is best to be cautious and feel your way around the group that you are with before introducing a topic for discussion, or expressing your point of view.

- You may want to steer clear of subjects such as race relations, apartheid or local politics in South Africa.

- Avoid comparing one city in South Africa with another. South Africans are very proud of their own cities and they do not react well when told that one city is better than another.

Appropriate Social Behavior:

While behavioral patterns in South Africa largely parallel those of Great Britain due to its colonial past, you would look towards other cultures for guidance when it comes to appropriate behavior in certain ethnic groupings of the South African population (e.g., Indian and the Muslim population).

For those of you from a *Latino* background, a cautionary word. South Africans are punctual. They consider lateness as a sign of rudeness. If you have a legitimate reason for being late to a social engagement or business meeting, do phone ahead and explain the reason for your delay.

To the South African, the concept of family is extremely important. The Indigenous African peoples, and the more traditional Afrikaans culture, consider their extended family to be almost as important as the nuclear family. The English-speaking White community, however, place more emphasis on the nuclear family. Whichever culture you will be interacting with, remember that elderly people are viewed as wise in South Africa. Make sure that you always treat them with the utmost respect, even if they are not well known to you. Failure to show proper respect to the elderly could be your downfall in any social or business relationship.

Women can expect to encounter some sexist behavior in the official and business arena, being tested in ways that a male colleague would not. Take any snide remarks in your stride. Rather than displaying hostility, prove yourself by displaying your competency and you'll eventually gain everyone's respect.

If you think that a hand gesture is rude in your own country, chances are that it will also be rude in South Africa. Extend your arm and wave towards yourself if you want to call someone to you, rather than pointing. If you wish to say that everything is OK, a thumbs up is appropriate. Giving someone the "V" for victory sign is considered an obscene gesture. Yawning without covering your mouth, chewing with your mouth open and sniffling are considered improper.

Gift Giving Etiquette:

Although gift giving is not such a big deal in South Africa, you would never arrive in someone's home empty handed. Bringing your host a gift shows good manners and an appreciation for their hospitality. If you're time poor, then at the very least bring along a box of chocolates or a lovely bottle of wine. Beautifully wrapped gifts, such as flowers, fine liquor, or souvenirs from your country are all great gift ideas too.

It's unnecessary to go overboard with expensive gifts in South Africa, as you'll only succeed in making your host uncomfortable. A good rule of thumb is to spend no more than US$50.

Do give and receive gifts with both hands, particularly when giving a gift to a Muslim or Indian in South Africa, as the left hand is considered unclean.

Unlike other countries, there are no taboos associated with the giving of specific flowers in South Africa, except for carnations, which are often used at funerals.

Unlike other countries, there are no taboos associated with the giving of specific flowers in South Africa, except for carnations, which are often used at funerals.

Dining Etiquette:

"The real fact is that I could no longer stand their eternal cold mutton."

– CECIL RHODES, ENGLISH-BORN BUSINESSMAN, MINING MAGNATE, AND POLITICIAN IN SOUTH AFRICA (ON WHY HE LEFT ENGLAND FOR SOUTH AFRICA).

So, you've arrived in South Africa, you've made friends with some of the locals, and you've just been invited to a *braai*. What's a *braai*?

The word *braaivleis,* or *braai* for short, is Afrikaans for "roasted meat," and refers to a barbecue by the pool, a typical South African social event. The majority of South Africans are fond of their meat, so if you are vegetarian, do let your hosts know ahead of time. Don't make the mistake of arriving without alerting your host of your dietary requirements because of not wanting to inconvenience them, or worse, assume that there will be plenty of other options there for you. On the contrary, they'll be annoyed with you for not speaking up.

Prior to attending a *braai*, it's always a good idea to ask the hostess what the dress code is if you're unsure of what to wear. Depending on the socio-economics of the group that you will be mixing with, "casual dress" in South Africa may not be as relaxed as in Australia or the United States. And even though the atmosphere at a *braai* is a very informal one, always be punctual and don't forget to bring a gift for your hosts.

Because of the whole social construct in South Africa, most homes have domestic help, so it may not be necessary for you to extend your assistance with the preparations in the kitchen. Play it by ear. If your host or hostess is attending to most of the food preparation themselves, it wouldn't hurt to make the offer. Only offer to bring a salad or a dish to share with all those attending if you know your hosts well enough.

Due to its cultural diversity, South African table manners can vary depending on the ethnic group that you are with. If you are dining with South Africans of European or English descent, then even a burger might be cut up with a fork and knife. In this case, the knife would be kept in the right hand, the fork in the left. Refrain from pointing or waving hands around while holding the silverware and speaking. To indicate that you're still eating, cross your knife and fork on your plate. When you're done eating, place your knife and fork together on your plate.

If you are dining with South Africans of Indian descent, then food may be eaten with the hands, in which case dining etiquette for India should be followed. Eating is done with the right hand as the left hand is considered unclean. Remember never to pass or receive anything with your left hand, and refrain from licking your fingers or sampling the food from someone else's plate. Eat smaller portions of food at the beginning of your meal as you will be offered more food later on, and it's only good manners for you to accept. Not finishing everything on your plate will not cause offense either, although you may want to wait until everyone has finished before getting up to wash your hands.

If you are entering a Muslim home in South Africa, it is important to remove your shoes and leave them at the door. Although the more Westernized households may dine Continental style (knife and fork), the majority of Muslims take their food from a common plate in the center of the table, where people scoop up *hummus* (a Levantine Arab dip made from chickpeas) and other foodstuff with pita bread. Remember that eating and passing food must always be done with the right hand, as the left hand is generally regarded as unclean.

Dressing Etiquette:

Typical western dress is worn in the more urban parts of South Africa. Although dress and behavior tends to be more relaxed, it doesn't mean that all cultural sensitivity should be thrown out the window. Anything too short, too tight, or too revealing, is considered inappropriate dress in South Africa. Sneakers or shorts are only appropriate for the beach, pool, taking a walk, or going to a barbecue, never for walking around the city centre or sightseeing.

When invited to a barbecue, or *braai,* at someone's home, remember that the term "casual dress" in major cities like Johannesburg may be dressier than in other parts of the country. Jeans and shorts may not always be appropriate. Check with your hosts in advance to avoid embarrassment on both sides.

For more official social engagements, smart casual clothes for women are always a good idea (e.g., dresses, or skirts and smart tops).

Although bikinis are acceptable swimwear for the beach or pool, do bring a cover-up for when you get out of the water. And for all you naturalists out there, resist the temptation to sun bake topless or in the nude unless you are at a designated nudist beach.

Regarding tribal dress, the wearing of traditional dress by an African does not indicate a lack of education or an unfamiliarity with the ways of the world. Rather, it shows pride in their tribal identity. However, it is not appropriate for a foreign guest to dress in tribal clothing unless you have been invited to do so.

Safari Etiquette:

The word *safari* derives from the Swahili word for "journey," and refers to a trip on land for the purpose of viewing, photographing, and experiencing animals in their natural habitats. Thankfully, with greater laws for the preservation of many animal species, fewer people undertake a *safari* to hunt.

The game drives go for about three hours, beginning at 5 or 5:30 in the morning, and then again at 4pm. The time in between is when the sun is at its highest and the animals tend to rest. This is also your time, as a guest, to eat, rest and then eat some more. There are also stops for refreshments while on game drives. On the morning drives, the ranger and tracker may stop to serve coffee and some muffins. On the afternoon drives as the sun is going down, you may be served a choice of alcoholic and non-alcoholic beverages and appetizers.

Rule of thumb on *safari* is to maintain always respect for your guides, the wildlife, and the environment. On *safari*, you are at nature's mercy, surrounded by wild animals that can turn on you in a heartbeat. Your guides are the experts on animal behavior so follow their directions and trust their judgment unquestion-ingly. Keeping seated, quiet, and still is imperative to your safety when viewing wild animals. Never imitate animal sounds, throw objects at an animal, or corner a wild animal. You could be plac-ing yourself, as well as your group, in danger.

Respect the environment and appreciate the privilege of being on *safari*. If you bring any food in with you, make sure you take all the rubbish back with you too. Never feed it to the animals or litter the reserve. Never smoke while on *safari*.

To show your appreciation, do tip the rangers $10 per guest each day. If you are in a private vehicle, tip $20 per guest each day. Tip staff members at the lodge such as valets, butlers, waiters, and cleaners $5 each per day as their salaries are barely enough to live on.

Dressing for Safari:

Deciding what clothing to take for a week on *safari* can be tricky when you don't know what conditions to expect. The rule of thumb for a six-day *safari* is to take three changes of clothes with you, plus your own detergent for hand washing a few basics like T-shirts, socks, and underwear. Service staff at the lodges will generally not wash underwear for you as it is considered too intimate an item.

Basic items that you should bring to a *safari* should include the following:

- Long-sleeved shirts (preferably with sun-protection built into the cloth), sweats with hoods, cotton scarves, and other layers that you can pull on or shed off as the day heats up or cools down.

- Pants that zip off and turn into shorts are a great idea.

- Although camouflage colors may sound like a practical choice for safari, camouflage colored clothes are illegal in many African countries. The reason for this is that it causes serious problems with the military at border crossings or in airports. Tan and lighter colors are always acceptable.

To be on the safe side, do ask your tour organizer for guidance in this department.

- Many lodges have pools, so you may want to bring your swimmers and a cover-up.

- In case the weather turns, a lightweight raincoat or jacket may serve you well.

- Avoid bringing jeans as they take a long time to dry if they get wet.

- Sunglasses, sunscreen, and a hat with a front and back brim to shield you from the African sun are essential. A baseball cap will not quite do the job.

- Comfortable walking shoes and socks are essential to protect you from thorns and mosquito bites. Rubber flip-flops or sandals can be worn back at the lodge.

- Lastly, don't forget your camera. A safari is a photographer's paradise, so make sure yours has a large memory card, as you'll be clicking away all day.

Here are a couple of websites that will help you plan your safari wardrobe essentials:

ExOfficio – www.exofficio.com

Sportsman's Warehouse – www.sportsmanswarehouse.com

Safety Precautions:

You will get different reports on safety in South Africa from different sections of society. The fact is that there is still a high level of serious crime in South Africa, with most of the locals and foreign tourists having been touched by violence in some way, shape, or form. Always seek local advice about which areas are safe to visit, and which areas to avoid.

To be on the safe side, steer clear of the townships and outskirts unless you are with a local guide. You may also want to avoid the city centers at night, particularly the train stations. The inner suburbs of Johannesburg (Berea and Hillbrow) and the beach-front in Durban are particularly prone to crime.

As you would if you were traveling through major cities in Europe or Asia, exercise vigilance in public places and always keep watch over your handbag and backpack. Stick to the main roads when walking around, or travel in a group. Avoid taking shortcuts along isolated beaches, lookouts, public parks and picnic areas, as these are areas where assaults have occurred. Assaults and robberies have also taken place on local commuter and metro trains between Johannesburg and Pretoria, as well as on commuter trains in Cape Town.

When driving, keep your car doors locked, windows up, and valuables out of sight. Refrain from rolling down your window when stopped at traffic lights, highway ramps or intersections, as thieves frequently pose as vendors or beggars. Similarly, drive around debris on the road rather than stopping to clear it.

There is also a luggage theft problem at Johannesburg and Cape Town airports, so *do* use the airport plastic wrapping service when available. Stay away from unsolicited assistance with transport when arriving at the airport in Johannesburg.

Beware of bogus internet friendship, dating, and marriage schemes that operate from some African countries. These scams result from connections made through internet dating schemes or chat rooms. Once a virtual friendship develops, the foreigner is asked by their "friend" or prospective marriage partner to send money to enable travel to your country. Once the money has been received, the relationship is usually terminated and the odds of recovering the money is between zero to none.

seventeen

Southeast Asia

> "To travel in Europe is to assume a foreseen inheritance; in Islam, to inspect that of a close and familiar cousin. But to travel in farther Asia is to discover a novelty previously unsuspected and unimaginable."
>
> **– LORD BYRON, ENGLISH ROMANTIC POET.**

Historic Influences:

Southeast Asia consists of the countries that are geographically south of China, east of India, and north of Australia. It can be further divided into two geographic sub-regions:

- Mainland Southeast Asia: Mainland Southeast Asia is comprised of Vietnam, Cambodia, Laos, Thailand, Malaysia, Myanmar (formerly Burma), and Singapore.

- Maritime Southeast Asia: This area is comprised of Malaysia (only the states of Sarawak and Sabah, aka East Malaysia), the Philippines, Brunei, East Timor, Singapore, and most of Indonesia.

To know the religion in a Southeast Asian country is to understand the country's culture and identity. The first religion in Southeast Asia was Animism, an ancient indigenous religion of both mainland and island Southeast Asia that held the belief that non-human entities, such as plants, rocks, or the ocean, are spiritual beings. In this respect they have similarities to the Australian Aborigines. Commonly found throughout agricultural, rice growing communities and hill tribes, Animism also entails the worship of ancestors. There is still evidence of this in modern Thailand, both in the cities and in rural areas, where each home will have erected a spirit house in the corner of the garden.

From the 1st–3rd centuries, Buddhism and Hinduism appeared in the Malayan Peninsula, Indonesia and southern delta regions of Thailand, Burma, and Cambodia.

From the 8th–13th centuries, Indian traders and missionaries from India and Ceylon introduced Hinduism to Cambodia and Indonesia. Hinduism saw the rise of the great Indonesian empires of Sri Vijaya, Malayu, Mataram, and Majapahit. In Cambodia, it was the basis of the ancient Angkorian civilization.

During the same timeframe, Theravada Buddhism became dominant in Thailand and southern Burma. Also known as the "Doctrine of the Elders", Theravada Buddhism is the school of Buddhism that draws its scriptural inspiration from the Tipitaka, which contains the earliest surviving record of the Buddha's teachings. Although Theravada Buddhism was eventually overtaken by the Khmer and the Thai, it eventually conquered its conquerors and spread throughout Burma in the 11th century, Thailand in the 13th–14th centuries, post Angkor Cambodia, as well as Laos.

While Islam had been present since the early Christian era among Muslim traders, it started to spread as a unified movement in the late 14th and early 15th centuries when the fall of Baghdad affected the trade routes and revenues of the Islamic world. Taking root strongly among the commercial groups in the port cities of Sumatra, Java, and southern Malay peninsula at Malacca, Islam later spread to eastern Indonesia.

Several upheavals in Java and Sumatra over a 200-year period saw the disorderly retreat of defeated Hindu troops and the establishment of a new polity, or municipality, in the various Islam states of Demak, Banten, Aceh and Mataram. The arrival of the Portuguese, Dutch, French, and British merchants, missionaries and administrators, pushed Islam to unite and cooperate in order to protect its gains from the new threat, as the counter-reformation spread to SE Asia.

Catholic Christianity first took hold in Goa, India, in the late 1400s, after Da Gama's discovery of the sea passage to the east. Quickly spreading to Malacca, Macao, and other ports, it made its first appearance in the Philippines in 1571, when the Spanish captured Manila. It rapidly spread throughout most of Lowland Luzon and the Visayas in the 1650s. Protestant Christianity made its appearance with the Dutch in the early 17th century, but it wasn't until the early 19th century that the Protestant missionaries started any work on converting the locals.

Today, Islam is the most widely practiced religion in Southeast Asia, with majorities in Brunei, Indonesia, and Malaysia. Numbering approximately 240 million, or 40% of the entire population, most Muslims in Southeast Asia belong to the Sunni sect.

The countries with a Theravada Buddhist majority are Thailand, Cambodia, Laos, and Burma. Mahayana Buddhism, a more liberal and accessible interpretation of Buddhism that includes the veneration of celestial beings such as Buddhas and bodhisattvas, is the predominant religion of the Chinese communities in Singapore. Vietnam continues to have a Mahayana Buddhist majority to this day. It is also represented by strong minorities in Malaysia, Brunei, the Philippines, and Indonesia.

Apart from the Philippine Catholics making up 80% of the population, and the Indonesian Protestant Christians making up 8%, Christianity has had comparatively little success in Southeast Asia. Having said that, Protestant missionary efforts have expanded into Java and Borneo in more recent times.

Greeting & Conversation Etiquette:

While the Western handshake has become prevalent in many countries of Southeast Asia, especially Malaysia, Vietnam, the Philippines, Singapore, and Indonesia, a handshake that is too firm will be interpreted as aggressive. So keep your grip soft in Southeast Asia.

The handshake is by no means universal, particularly since religious and cultural beliefs can vary from region to region. According to Muslim tradition, men and women do not touch if they are not related by blood or are married. This applies in countries such as Indonesia, Brunei, and Malaysia. In Thailand, a greeting called the *wai,* which resembles a prayerful gesture, is the official protocol. The safest bet would be to observe what others around you are doing, then follow suit.

First names are never used initially in Southeast Asian cultures. To do so would be a sign of disrespect. Even when enough familiarity has been established, wait to be given permission before doing so.

In parts of Southeast Asia, like Thailand, people may call a woman "sir" instead of "miss" or "ma'am." In the provinces of the Philippines, they may even refer to a woman as "Sir-Ma'am." Don't be insulted, or even try and correct them. Referring to someone as 'sir' is meant to be a sign of respect in parts of Southeast Asia.

In countries like Malaysia, Singapore, and Bali, where Muslim and Hindu cultures prevail, only the right hand is used in social interaction (e.g., eating, giving gifts, and making hand gestures). The left hand is considered unclean.

If you must point, do so with your right knuckle rather than the index finger, with the palm of your hand facing down. Pointing with your index finger will be considered disrespectful at best, and a sign of hostility at worse.

In all cultures in Southeast Asia, the elderly are valued and respected. Always acknowledge the elderly first when walking into a room. Repeat this ritual again when leaving.

Remember the advertisement for Singapore Airlines? Smiling, politeness, graciousness, and a self-deferring manner is a necessary part of Southeast Asian interaction. Adopting this behavior will get you the best results.

Raised voices, displays of anger and generally losing your cool, no matter how justified, is considered very bad form in Southeast Asia, where people are by and large gentle and discreet. Any over-the-top displays of temper or histrionics will lead to you being totally ignored, or viewed with disapproval. And when you've gone, you can guarantee that your behavior will be mocked and laughed at for a long time to come. Either way, it does not paint foreigners in a good light, and it will totally defeat your cause.

Conversation Taboos:

Southeast Asians are conservative. They do not appreciate conversations with any sexual overtones, even if it is in the form of a joke. Religion is also taken seriously, so any jokes on religion will be considered disrespectful, especially if your views are critical of Islam, Buddhism, or Catholicism.

Avoid criticizing the government in Southeast Asia. In addition to it being considered bad form in most countries, a disrespectful comment about the royal family in Thailand can actually cost you a fine.

Appropriate Social Behavior:

In the Buddhist tradition, the head is the holiest part of the body as it is the closest to the heavens. It is for this reason that one must never touch or pat a person's head in Southeast Asia, even a child's. While this belief is not prevalent in the Philippines, where the majority are Catholic, this is relevant for Thailand, Bali, Cambodia, Laos, Burma, and Malaysia.

While the head is the holiest part of the body, the feet are considered unclean. Avoid showing the soles of the feet, or pointing the soles of your feet towards other people, by sitting with your legs crossed out in front of you. Rather, you must tuck your legs sideways under the chair, or have your feet firmly on the ground. If you are seated on the ground, then tuck your legs underneath you, or sideways. Likewise, never step over someone's legs or feet. Shoes are to be removed before entering temples, and in some private homes. Again, while this belief is not prevalent in the Philippines, where the majority are Catholic, this is relevant for Thailand, Bali, Cambodia, Laos, Burma, and Malaysia.

More often than not, you will be subjected to children, or elderly people begging in Southeast Asia. This is not only difficult to witness, it can at times be heart rending, especially if you don't come from a country where this occurs. Callous as it sounds, avoid giving money, or even food, to beggars in Southeast Asia. Your generosity will only end up benefiting the local scammers, with little or none going to the beggars themselves. Give generously to reputable charities instead, and make sure that you buy your souvenirs directly from the local craftsmen. There are plenty of fake imports that are sold in souvenir shops that hardly benefit the local population or craft industry.

Always ask permission before taking a photo of any of the locals. If they oblige, then show them the photo afterwards and offer some sort of payment. This unwritten rule is applicable to any country in the world. Forget about the belief that you'll be taking away their spirit. It's just plain rude and does not afford the locals any sort of dignity. Just like you, they are not animals in a zoo.

Refrain from photographing a friend in front of a Buddha. Likewise, never take photographs with your back to the Buddha. This is considered highly disrespectful.

Although the European practice of kissing family and friends on the cheek and chaste hand holding is acceptable in the Philippines, any other excessive displays of affection, such as passionate kissing and groping in public, are a no-no in Southeast Asia. It is considered disrespectful and will earn you a stern reprimand for being offensive.

Gift Giving Etiquette:

When invited to someone's home in Southeast Asia, do follow the universal custom of bringing a gift for your host. However, in Southeast Asia, the color of the wrapping paper must be chosen carefully.

- In Singapore, do not use the colors white, blue, or black, which represents funerals.

- In Thailand, green, black, and blue are to be avoided, while yellow or gold is acceptable.

- In Indonesia, the colors red and gold are very lucky.

- In Cambodia, the color white is considered a color for mourning.

- Except for black, which represents death and mourning as in the West, the Philippines has no color taboos.

- Acceptable presents for your Southeast Asian host can include a beautiful handicraft from your country, or a coffee table book, and something for your host's children. Never give a sharp object as a gift, which can symbolize the cutting of the friendship.

The Philippines would be the only country where it would be acceptable to bring alcohol. However, it's always best to clarify if your hosts enjoy wine or spirits. Most Filipinos are not big drinkers.

Don't be hurt if your host puts your present aside after receiving it. Presents are opened after you leave so as not to hurt the feeling of the other guests, who may feel left out.

Apart from the Philippines, where bringing pastries to a lunch engagement in someone's home is acceptable, it's not a good idea to bring food as a gift in Southeast Asia. Bringing food implies that your host hasn't prepared adequately for you. You can either bring a beautifully presented box of chocolates, or send a luscious basket of fruit as a thank-you after the event.

Dining Etiquette:

In regions of Southeast Asia where Buddhism or Islam is prevalent, it is customary to leave one's shoes outside the front door before entering. Rule of thumb is that if you see shoes outside the door, leave yours behind too.

If you enter a dining room and see a series of low-lying tables and cushions, feel free to sit on the cushions and relax, remembering to tuck the soles of your feet away. This is frequently how the locals dine in Thailand.

In the international homes or higher end restaurants of Southeast Asia, Continental style dining (with fork and knife) may be used. However, the most common way to dine in Thailand, the Philippines, Indonesia, and Bali, is with a spoon and fork. When eating with a spoon and fork, it is not considered good form for the spoon to make noise as it hits your teeth. Southeast Asians are very delicate when they eat, using their lips, rather than their teeth, to make contact with the spoon.

In Vietnam, and with Southeast Asians of Chinese decent, chopsticks are used for eating.

Here are some things to remember when eating with chopsticks:

Hold your chopstick closer to the thicker end at the top, not in the middle or all the way towards the front (slimmer end).

Never stick your chopsticks into your food, and especially not into the rice. The practice of sticking chopsticks into the rice is reserved for funerals, when rice is placed at the altar.

Remember that your chopsticks are not a conductor's baton or magic wand that you wave around in the air while speaking, nor is it something that you spear food with, move bowls and plates around with, or drum on the tables.

Passing food from your set of chopsticks to another's is a no-no, as this too is a funeral practice.

When you're serving yourself food from shared dishes, use the opposite end of your chopsticks (thicker end) to move some food from the shared plates onto your own if you have not already eaten from your chopsticks. Otherwise, use the serving chopsticks that may be provided for that purpose.

Do not drop your chopsticks, as it is considered bad luck.

Eating with your hand is a wonderfully sensual experience in some ethnic communities of Southeast Asia, with the food more than likely served on banana leaves. Firstly, make sure that you wash your hands before you start eating. Always use your right hand when handling your food, never the left. Rice is normally used as a base for the meal and is eaten with all the other dishes. Scoop small bits of rice together with the tips of your fingers, lower your head towards the food, and pop the food into your mouth delicately with your finger tips. The palm of your hand, or in fact any area above the knuckles, must not be used at all. Making slurping sounds, and licking your fingers, isn't considered polite.

Platters of a variety of dishes are often served in the middle of the table to share, in both restaurants or homes in Southeast Asia. Always defer to the oldest, or more senior person at the table, before serving yourself. Make sure that you don't use the utensil that you eat with to serve the food.

In some Thai and Chinese restaurants and households, it's customary not to flip the whole fish over after eating one side. Superstition states that flipping the fish causes the fishermen to flip their boats. Allow the waiter at your restaurant, or host, to carefully remove the bones so that you can continue eating the fish from the same side.

Always leave a small amount of food behind on your plate, as it shows that you've had more than enough to eat.

Although tipping is always appreciated in more up-market restaurants, it is not expected in casual restaurants and street stalls.

Dressing Etiquette:

Although one can be tempted to wear as little as possible due to the humidity and heat in Southeast Asia, remember that the Southeast Asians are very modest. Displaying a lot of skin, like your cleavage, navel, chests, shoulders, and bare legs, will attract a lot of stares and embarrass the locals. While it's okay to wear shorts and bathing suits around the beaches or resorts, avoid parading around in them once you have left the beach and resort grounds.

Regarding dress etiquette in temples, mosques and churches, cover up your arms, neckline, and legs – no shorts, and no cleavage showing, ladies, as any show of skin is considered offensive. Make sure that your blouse or dress has sleeves; even cap sleeves are not acceptable. Bring a wrap or a large scarf with you to cover your neck, shoulders and, in some places, your head. Some temples and mosques may refuse you entry unless your head is covered. To play it safe, just observe what the local women are wearing, and follow their example. Pants and skirts should be well below the knee.

Although many communities in Southeast Asia are not exactly affluent, Southeast Asians are meticulous about hygiene and neatness. They have an aversion to body odors and unkempt appearances. Looking scruffy and smelling badly signifies a lack of self-respect in Southeast Asia, which will ultimately affect the way that you will be treated.

Visiting Buddhist Temples:

No travel to East and Southeast Asia would be complete without a visit to a Buddhist temple. Considered "holy grounds," Buddhist temples have their own set of rules and etiquettes. The first thing you should do before visiting a temple is to check the schedule of the temple ahead of time to avoid interrupting meditation sessions and religious services.

Once you've arrived at the temple, you must remove your shoes and leave them at the entrance. This stems from the belief that the soles of the feet, and shoes, are considered unclean. To make it easier on yourself, try wearing slip-on shoes or sandals on the day that you will be visiting. Walking into a temple without removing your shoes is considered disrespectful, and failing to remove your shoes will lead to a reprimand, and sometimes being told to leave the premises.

You've arrived modestly dressed, you've left your shoes at the entrance, and you quietly shuffle behind the line of locals as they make their way into the temple. So far you've ticked all the boxes. What happens next?

Do as the locals do and bow your head in respect to the temple and the Buddha statues as you enter. This is the time to be quiet, respectful, and deferential. There are people meditating and praying around you and they will not appreciate being interrupted by tourists and noisy foreign guests.

Never point at or touch Buddha statues, images, monks, nuns, and elders, particularly on the head as it is considered the highest part of the body. Its also disrespectful to touch people on the head like one would a child. When standing in front of a statue of Buddha, always remember that the feet are considered the "lowest" part of the body, so it is considered very offensive if your toes point directly at the statue. Place your feet in a "V" shape, or have them pointing away instead.

A woman must never touch a monk, a monk's robes, sit next to a monk, or hand anything directly to the monk. If you want to hand something to a monk, it is best to place it within his reach. And when meeting a Buddhist monk or nun, the proper way to greet them is by putting the palms of your hands together and raising them to your chin while bowing your head slightly. Never shake their hands, particularly with members of the opposite sex.

Regarding any public displays of affection, Asians have a very modest outlook on this at the best of times, so save any hugging, kissing, or holding hands with your spouse or partner until you're back at your hotel room. A sacred temple is not the place for it.

Regarding your children, it's terrific that you want to expose them to different cultural experiences. However, a temple is not the ideal place for you to take a toddler, for the simple reason that they tend to be noisy and restless. It may be a better idea for one of you to stay outside with them while the other goes inside. Only bring your children inside the temple with you if they are mature, well-behaved, and you can keep them under control. Running around, raising their voices, leaning and climbing over the statues, or getting too close to the monks, nuns or images will be frowned upon and will earn them (and you) a severe reprimand. And finally, eating and drinking in the temple is considered completely unacceptable.

And finally, small monetary contributions are always welcome, as are offerings of food and supplies to the temple's monks, nuns, and Lamas.

Visiting Mosques:

Similar to the etiquette when visiting Buddhist temples, dress modestly when visiting a mosque. Showing too much skin will cause great offense. Have a scarf in your bag so that you may cover your head before entering. Remember to leave your shoes outside. Unless you are Muslim, you will not be permitted to enter the mosque's main prayer hall. Avoid visiting a mosque between 11am and 2pm on Friday, which is considered the Sabbath day.

As a sign of respect, put your cameras and video recorders away, and turn your mobile phones off, before entering a mosque.

Safety Precautions:

Remember that Southeast Asians are extremely modest, not just in the way that they dress but also in their behavior. Public displays of affection, apart from chaste hand holding, is considered offensive, so adopt modest dress and behavior in Southeast Asia. To do otherwise would bring the wrong kind of attention to yourself, leaving you vulnerable to scammers and thieves.

Despite the seeming ease with which drugs can be bought in this part of the world, avoid the temptation completely. Drugs are illegal in Southeast Asia, and the penalty for carrying drugs in some nations is punishable by death.

Keep your wits about you and avoid drinking excessively in public. Do not accept food and drinks from strangers, or leave your food and drink unattended, as drink 'spiking' is common.

In Singapore, chewing gum is illegal and you can be fined heavily for just spitting, loitering and jaywalking.

Be careful of any region where there is political turmoil. Stay away from any protests or demonstrations, however peaceful they may seem, as they have the potential to turn violent without warning.

Be aware that prostitution is widespread in Southeast Asia, with the 'flesh trade' assuming the dimensions of a commercial sector. As disadvantaged locals strive for a better life by selling their children into the industry, prostitution has very serious implications relating to social welfare, transmission of HIV/AIDS, criminality, violations of the basic human rights of commercial sex workers, and commercial sexual exploitation especially of children.

eighteen

Spain

"Anything you can imagine is real."

– PABLO PICASSO, GREAT SPANISH PAINTER.

Historic Influences:

Located in south western Europe, Spain occupies the Iberian Peninsula, and is bathed by the Mediterranean Sea, the Atlantic Ocean and the Cantabrian Sea.

First inhabited around 8,000 BC, Spain's ideal geographical location made it attractive to foreign powers, beginning from the 11th century BC, when it was colonized by the Phoenicians, then the Greeks and the Carthaginians.

The year 218 BC saw the arrival of the Romans, who fought the Carthaginians in what was known as the Second Punic War. Harvesting the peninsula's agricultural and mineral wealth, they established sophisticated cities with aqueducts, temples and theaters.

As the Roman Empire teetered towards collapse in the early 5th century AD, Visigothic invaders from the North took control over Spain. Due to their lack of political organization, however, the Visigoths were ousted by the Moors from North Africa, who took over the entire Iberian Peninsula in the 8th century. Calling their new civilization "Al Andalus," Spain became the rich soil in which mathematics, geography, astronomy and poetry flourished. By the 9th and 10th centuries, Cordoba was Europe's leading city.

Northern Christian kingdoms attempted to re-conquer "Al Andalus" from the Moors in the 11th century, as the marriage of Catholic Monarchs Fernando Aragon and Isabel of Castile inspired Spanish unity. Taking Granada, the last Moorish kingdom, in 1492, the Monarchs rejoiced when Columbus discovered America in the same year, opening the way for the riches from the New World.

However, Spain's misfortunes started when the vast riches from the New World were squandered by the Habsburg dynasty in endless foreign wars. Made worse by high inflation and religious oppression, her doom continued into the next century with an invasion by Napoleon and the loss of the American colonies.

Defeat brought a new radicalism to Spain, as a strong Anarchist movement began to emerge in the 19th and early 20th centuries. The chaotic conditions eventually led to a dictatorship, and a republic in the 1930s. This was later destroyed by the Spanish Civil War, after which General Franco ruled by repression until his death in 1975. From that day onwards, Spain has been a democracy.

Greeting & Conversation Etiquette:

Spaniards are aggressive and animated conversationalists, making good use of hand gestures. It is not uncommon for numerous people to speak simultaneously in a group setting. In their eyes, it's the most effective weapon against not being heard.

Spaniards normally stand very close to the person with whom they are speaking with. It's okay, you will get used to it in time. It's important to maintain eye contact during any conversation with a Spaniard, no matter how drastic the surrounding distractions. You'll be perceived as rude, distracted, or disinterested if you don't.

The people of Spain are polite and tend to be on the formal side when you first meet them, so defer to European formalities when addressing someone that you have newly met, addressing them as *Señor* (Mr), *Señora* (Mrs), or *Señorita* (Ms) followed by their surname, until such time as you have been given permission to use their first names.

Spanish women usually meet and part with a small hug and a beso on each cheek when meeting close friends and family members. *Besos,* or kisses, tend to be just air-kisses. If you're a tad confused as to when to *besar,* wait for someone to instigate it first.

The word *usted* (abbreviated as *ud*) is a more formal version of *tu,* meaning "you." It is widely used in business, or as a sign of respect to the elderly or person of seniority.

The Spanish are very well traveled, and welcome conversation topics regarding your travels, art, architecture, Spanish tradition, food, wines, and especially soccer or football. You are also welcome to discuss politics with care and sensitivity, and only if you know what you are talking about.

The family is important to the Spaniards, so inquiring about the welfare of family members will put you in their good books. Spaniards will welcome any conversation about your family members too.

Conversation Taboos:

- Spaniards are a very proud race and take offense to criticism about their country or customs. And with a cultural emphasis on honor and personal pride comes little appreciation for self-deprecating humor. They will never understand the need to belittle one's achievements, nor appreciate it if you tease them about theirs.

- Even if you disagree with the practice, avoid having a conversation or debate about bullfighting. Bullfighting is an ancient tradition in Spain, bullfighters are still considered national heroes, and the country is torn at the moment between those who are for it and those who are opposed to it.

- Avoid any discussion on religion, Franco, the Civil War and WWII, Basque separatism and Catalan regionalism.

- Avoid enquiries of a personal nature during first introductions, as this will be considered invasive.

Appropriate Social Behavior"

Time is very relaxed in Spain. *Nos vemos a las ocho* ("We'll see each other at eight") could mean 8:00, 8:15, 8:30, or even later. Spaniards are often late and it is not considered rude. However, if you have an appointment with a doctor, or have a business meeting, you must arrive on time, even if you are kept waiting for a long time.

If you want to get together with a friend for a social chat, it is customary to invite them for a *cafecito* ("little coffee"). On your first date with a Spanish man, it is always a good idea to go out in a group first, until you know and trust him.

Males cross their legs in a social setting while women cross their ankles. Despite their Arab roots, the Spanish do not have the same issue with the soles of the feet that other cultures have. However, they will understandably draw the line on you putting your feet on the furniture.

Spaniards will frown at chewing gum or keeping your hands in your pockets while you are in a public setting. They feel that it looks cheap and slovenly.

Pushing and shoving while waiting in line for a bus or a taxi is common practice in some situations and circles. Remember that the Spanish concept of space is different to that of most people from Anglo-Saxon cultures.

Machismo is alive and well in places like Andalucía, where women may be the object of whistling and catcalling when walking alone or in groups without any men. It's best to ignore this behavior as it is harmless.

If you pull down on your bottom eyelid in Spain, you are insinuating to "be alert" or that "I am alert." In Spain, crossing you fingers means "good luck," and is considered a friendly gesture. Otherwise, any other hand gesture that is considered offensive in your own country will be offensive in Spain too.

Dining Etiquette:

"We don't grow older, we grow riper."

– PABLO PICASSO, GREAT SPANISH PAINTER.

A major part of appreciating Spanish culture is about savoring the rusticity and richness of their cuisine. The Spanish take their food and wine very seriously, so if you want to fully assimilate, you should too. Spanish cuisine is comprised of the expansive regional flavors of Galicia, Castilia, Valencia, the Basque Regions, and the rest of the Mediterranean.

Breakfast and dinner are smaller meals for the Spanish, while the midday meal is the largest. Breakfast is usually eaten on the run at a bar, and is nothing more elaborate than a milky coffee and a sweet roll or croissant. At about 10am , the locals might leave the office for a plate of *churros con chocolate,* curls of fried doughnut-like batter eaten with hot melted chocolate.

Lunch is eaten between 1:30 and 4pm, and is the main meal of the day. Most restaurants will offer a lunchtime menu called *Menu del Dia,* which consists of a fixed three-course meal plus a house wine. You can pay extra for a better wine if you want to. Priced at between 8-16 Euros, this fixed meal makes it possible to enjoy high-quality meals at some of the best restaurants in town at reasonable prices. As lunchtime is the main meal of the day, and dinner is not usually served until after 9pm, you may want to take full advantage of the siesta hour and have a nap.

Dinner is eaten between 9pm and 11pm. Eating dinner any earlier will single you out as a foreign tourist. Dinner is a lighter meal consisting of *tapas,* or a *sopa* (soup) and salad.

Tapas relate to the snacks, canapés or finger food available in just about every Spanish bar, and are a national institution. In the Basque region, they are called *pintxos* (pronounced pin-CHOS). Costing just a few Euros apiece, the trick is to give yourself a limit of two to three *tapas* per bar before moving on to the next bar for the next round. There are the cold *tapas,* displayed at the bar on trays, and the hot *tapas,* made to order. The two-to-three-*tapas*-per-bar rule is easier said than done, though, as they truly are a taste sensation. Most bars operate on an honor system, where you let the bar man know how many *tapas* or *pintxos* you have consumed, and pay for it at the end with your wine. However, many Spanish barmen tend not to trust tourists and ask that you pay as you consume.

Paella is a dish that originated from Valencia, Spain. Its main ingredients are rice, saffron, and a combination of seafood, chicken, and/or pork. The best *paellas* in Spain are not found in restaurants but in people's homes. However, if you are hell-bent on having one, do yourself a favor and ask the locals where you can find the best *paella* in town. Restaurants that cater to tourists will not serve you anything better than a microwavable dish of yellow rice with lots of salt and a few mussels thrown in, and will charge you plenty for it to boot.

In urban Spain, it is far more common for friends and colleagues to meet for *tapas* for dinner than to go to a restaurant or a dinner party at someone's home. But if you do get the chance to be seated at the table, watch your table manners, as the Spanish are very particular about them.

Eating in Spain is done Continental style, which means that the fork is held in the left hand and the knife in the right. Refrain from resting your elbows on the table. Hands should be visible and not on your lap. There isn't a set time to toast your Spanish host, so the start of the meal should be fine. A simple *salud* (good health) will suffice.

Never cut salad with a knife and fork or pick up the lettuce with your hand. Rather, fold the lettuce on to your fork before bringing it to your mouth, delicately. Fruit should be peeled and sliced before eating it. Resist the temptation to pick fruit up with your fingers. Save that for the countryside.

If you are still hungry, place your fork on one side of your empty plate and your knife on the other. This signals that you would like to be served some more. However, a clean plate is expected in Spain so do not order any more than you are able to consume. When you have finished eating, place your knife and fork together on the bottom right hand side of your plate. Leave your wineglass nearly full if you do not want your wine glass refilled.

When you have finished eating in company, even strangers, you must say *Buen provecho* or *Que aproveche* (good eating). This is answered with *gracias* (thank you). Do stay and socialize for a few hours after finishing your meal. Otherwise, your host may feel that you were there only for a free feed.

When dining at a restaurant, be friendly to your Spanish waiter. Give him or her some extra *kudos* whenever you have the opportunity, as they will give you better service for it and make some marvelous recommendations. Then again, you may get the occasional Spanish waiter that just doesn't like tourists, like the waiter that we struck in Toledo. In that case, just leave out the tip.

Gift Giving Etiquette:

The family is considered to be the most important part of any Spaniard's life. To be invited to the family home for a meal, particularly for Sunday lunch, is an honor. It's considered good form to bring along a present for the host. Chocolates, pastries, a bottle of fine brandy or whisky, or flowers are good presents to bring with you. Handicrafts or coffee table books that represent your country and culture will also be appreciated as gifts. As the Spanish love their children, you'll gain credit by bringing sports team shirts and caps for your host's children.

Always make sure your gift is beautifully wrapped and presented. If you are given a present by a Spaniard, you should open it immediately in front of the giver.

When bringing flowers, do not bring dahlias, chrysanthemums, white lilies, or red roses. The first three varieties are used for funerals while red roses are a romantic gesture. Always give flowers in odd numbers, except for 13, which is an unlucky number.

Dressing Etiquette:

Like most Europeans, the Spanish put a lot of emphasis on grooming and dressing well, so it is important for you to project good taste and a sense of fashion. Dressing for comfort in Spain (e.g., tracksuit and runners) will only draw attention to you for all the wrong reasons, and you will not be taken seriously. And while Spain is known for its soaring temperatures in the summer, avoid flashy colors or wearing shorts unless you are at the beach.

Like the French and the Italians, the Spaniards believe that fewer items of clothing that are well-made and of the best quality is far better than a large wardrobe filled with cheap clothes. So long as your wardrobe is neat and of a high quality, do not worry about wearing the same thing too often. You will fit right in.

Shoes are the most scrutinized aspect of anyone's wardrobe in Spain, men and women, so make sure that yours are carefully shined, up-to-date in fashion, and of a good quality.

Do dress up for restaurants and clubs. The bar area of restaurants are always more casual, while everyone dresses up for the formal dining area. To be on the safe side, you may want to find out ahead of time if you will be going out for *tapas* or formal dining.

Women with bare shoulders should carry a shawl or wrap when touring churches and monasteries. It is considered disrespectful to wear shorts or short skirts in these places.

Safety Precautions:

Petty crime, such as pick-pocketing and bag snatching, is particularly common in tourist areas and on public transport in large Spanish cities, especially Madrid, Barcelona, Valencia and Seville. The thieves are light fingered and highly skilled at stealing valuables, including passports and money, without attracting the owner's attention.

Thieves often work in gangs and use various diversionary tactics to distract the attention of tourists. For example, they may use large maps or offer assistance to distract a traveler's attention, while an accomplice steals the traveler's valuables. Thieves can sometimes pose as plain clothes policemen, stealing money and credit cards from tourists' wallets as they check the tourist's identification.

Be extra vigilant with your ATM cards. Only use machines in protected environments, such as banks, department stores, and shopping centers. Tourists are sometimes intimidated into providing the pin number for their ATM card.

Never leave your food and drink unattended, as drink "spiking," followed by theft or sexual assault, have been reported. Similarly, never accept food and drinks from a stranger.

Keep your windows up and doors locked when inside a vehicle. Don't fall for strangers wanting you to pull over because of an apparent problem with your vehicle, or offer assistance to change a slashed or flat tire. While one assists you, an accomplice steals from the car. Never leave anything of value in your car. Cars with foreign number plates are especially targeted.

[n i n e t e e n]
The Caribbean

"How-de-do and thank you break no square." (Translates to: "It is not only good manners to be polite, it does no harm")

– OLD JAMAICAN PROVERB

Historic Influences:

Archaeological carbon dating place the arrival of the first humans in the Caribbean between 3,500 and 4,000 BC. Migrating from North America, Central America, and the Northern region of South America, the *Arawak* populated the larger Caribbean Islands of Cuba, Hispaniola, Jamaica, and Puerto Rico, while the *Carib* lived on the smaller volcanic islands of the eastern Caribbean: St. Kitts-Nevis, Antigua, Guadeloupe, Dominica, Martinique, St. Lucia, Barbados, St. Vincent and Tobago.

In 1492, Christopher Columbus landed on a small island he called San Salvador. He died believing he had reached the east by sailing west, and that he had landed on the islands southwest of India. This is how the islands of the Caribbean became known as the West Indies.

As the news of the "new world" spread across Europe like wildfire, everyone wanted a piece of the action. With the British, French and Dutch joining the Spaniards as conquistadors, outbreaks of diseases like measles and smallpox, which the Europeans brought with them, quickly spread and decimated the local population.

Between 1630 and 1640, the Dutch took control of Aruba, Bonaire, Curacao, Saint Eustatius, Saint Martin and Saba. The British claimed Antigua, Barbados and Nevis, and the French Martinique and Guadeloupe. Eventually, European colonization resulted in the almost complete depopulation of the West Indies native populations.

In the 1640s, Portuguese Jews emigrated from Brazil to Barbados, taking with them the techniques of cultivating sugar cane, which led to the establishment of the sugar cane plantations, some of which are operational today. With sugar came slavery, with an estimated 10 million slaves being brought from Africa to work on the plantations, thus repopulating the region. Working in horrific conditions, the slaves were provided mainly by the Dutch and English traders.

With African slaves quickly outnumbering the Europeans and Native Americans, rebellions became common. The costs of maintaining slavery and enforcing order began to skyrocket. This led to many Europeans to pressure their governments into abolishing slavery. Led by Denmark, which abolished the slave trade in 1803, Britain followed in 1807, France in 1817, Holland in 1818, Spain in 1820, and Sweden in 1824. Slavery was abolished in the British colonies in 1833–34, in the French colonies in 1838, in the Dutch colonies in 1863, and in the Spanish colonies of Puerto Rico in 1873 and Cuba in 1880.

After emancipation in the British colonies, plantation labor eventually came from India, as indentured servants were attracted by contracts that paid their passage, and offered them options that included the acquisition of land.

Greeting & Conversation Etiquette:

Although English is understood in most nations and islands of the Caribbean, you'll win the respect of the locals by learning some conversational Spanish or French when visiting regions where these languages are spoken.

You may greet people with a smile and a hearty "good morning," "good afternoon," or "good evening." As patience, tolerance and generosity are highly valued in the Caribbean, the phrases "please" and "thank you" are regularly expressed. You are also expected to greet service providers like restaurant and bar staff, shop assistants, hotel staff, and taxi drivers, as well as acknowledge anyone that you might pass by on the street. I told you the locals were friendly.

The most common greeting in the Caribbean is a handshake with direct eye contact and a warm smile. However, avoid shaking the hand with a vice-like grip as it will not impress the locals. This is not a *macho* culture, and such an outward display of strength and assertiveness is not necessary in the Caribbean, where a softer grip is the norm. When shaking hands with ladies, men will often wait for the lady to offer her hand first. Hugging and kissing is reserved only for close friends and family members.

Address people by the title Mr, Mrs, or Miss and their surname. Wait until invited before using someone's first name. As your friendship develops, you may even be asked to call the person by their nickname. The elderly are highly respected in the Caribbean, so make a point of showing a certain degree of respect to them.

Some Westerners are surprised to find that most people of the Caribbean do not smile readily, often appearing even standoffish, in the initial introduction. This might seem at odds with the perception of people living in a tropical paradise. However, the people of the Caribbean adopted some of the behavior of their colonizers, the French and the British, who traditionally remain reserved until they develop a trust and familiarity with someone. Similarly, most of the people of the Caribbean will show a reserved face until they get to know the person better and develop a trust. But once that trust has been earned, they are naturally warm, welcoming, generous, and easygoing.

Knowing that family and respect for seniority are commonplace in the Caribbean, make a point of introducing the most senior people present first in any gathering It is important to show deference and respect. You will commonly hear someone referred to as "bossman" or "bosswoman."

The people of the Caribbean are very direct when speaking, saying what they mean and meaning what they say. They will expect you to be equally direct. At the same time, they do value tact, sensitivity and good manners. They are polite even when they have to disagree with you. They abhor overt aggression, though, so tone it down several notches if you have the tendency to get fired up in a debate or discussion.

The Caribbean *patois,* a non-standard language that mixes phrases and words from other languages, is called "Creole.". It evolved hundreds of years ago when slaves had to find a way to communicate with their European plantation owners. If you have difficulty understanding the Creole *patois,* simply ask politely whether the speaker could repeat himself or herself. Never ask to be spoken to "properly,", as any reference to English being the "superior" language is considered disrespectful. Since some of the words and phrases are in English, one can usually get the gist of what is being said.

Conversation Taboos:

- The people of the Caribbean are family-orientated, have a healthy respect for women and the elderly, and view religion – primarily Christianity – as an inherent part of their lives. Avoid discussions on religion if your views happen to be disparaging.

- Steer clear of any swearing, discussions on sex, or telling any risqué jokes. You will be viewed as obnoxious and rude rather than funny or amusing.

- Steer clear of any political discussion, especially if it is disparaging, particularly in Cuba. Cuban citizens have restrictions placed on their freedom of speech, and right to convene an assembly, so distance yourself from any political activity while in the Caribbean.

Appropriate Social Behavior:

"If crab don' walk 'bout 'e won't get fat."

– OLD CARIBBEAN SAYING (MEANING THAT YOU ACCOMPLISH NOTHING BY STAYING AT HOME).

The people of the Caribbean prefer to put their faith in those they know well, such as their extended family and close friends, rather than someone in authority. Indeed, the family, and extension of it, is the most important group a person can belong to, and trust. This is the reason why people from this part of the world will look towards friends and neighbors first to pull together accumulated funds when buying a house or business, rather than approaching a banking institution. This is particularly common in Jamaica. Although one can be accepted as part of the extended family in the Caribbean, it is important to first earn their trust.

Apart from their intense love and loyalty for family and friends, the people of the Caribbean are also some of the most racially tolerant people of the world. Little wonder when you have a multitude of nationalities and races running through their veins.

In this part of the world, people stand very close when conversing, with men touching the arm or shoulder of another man, or even finger his shirt or jacket lapel while speaking. This is a sign of familiarity, trust, and is normal behavior.

When taking public transport, be prepared to give up your seat for pregnant women, the elderly, disabled, or mothers with infants or toddlers. Leave the seats closest to the bus doors for those that need them.

Be mindful of the conservative influence of the Church in Caribbean life, which heavily influences public behavior and outlook on homosexuality. Although public displays of affection between members of the opposite sex – hugging, handholding and a modest kiss – are acceptable, "passionate" displays of affection will be viewed as vulgar and may invoke intervention from the authorities. Similarly, although homosexuality is not illegal, there is still much intolerance towards it, with any public displays of affection attracting unwanted attention from the authorities.

In Jamaica, you may become fascinated by the Rastafarians because of the exotic and colorful way that they dress. However, remember that they are not a tourist attraction. If you would like to photograph them, approach your subject politely and ask them if they would mind if you took a picture of them.

When doing business in the Caribbean, avoid being confrontational, aggressive, or using high-pressure sales tactics. Forming long-term relationships are far more important. Business is hierarchical, and the person with the most authority makes all the decisions. Make sure that you always defer to the person with the most authority.

Dining Etiquette:

The people of the Caribbean love their food. Made up of an exotic blend of spices and bursting with flavors due to a vibrant fusion of cultural influences, dining is at the centre of all social and business get-togethers. When you're not being invited to someone's home, you'll be sampling some of the local cuisine at a restaurant.

When invited to a dinner party or lunch in someone's home, similarities with the British and French social practices end when it comes to punctuality in the Caribbean. The people here subscribe to "island time," arriving up to 30 minutes after the invited time. Table manners and ways of serving food are also relatively informal, with a preference for buffet-style.

Table manners are Continental, meaning that the fork is held in the left hand and the knife in the right. Do not sit down until you are invited to, and do ask the host where he or she would like you to be seated. Wait until everyone is seated and you're invited to start eating before digging into your food. Try a bit of everything as it shows graciousness, but be careful of how much you serve yourself as it is considered polite to finish everything on your plate. The flavors are wonderful so this won't exactly be a chore for you.

Gift Giving Etiquette:

The people of the Caribbean are some of the warmest, most hospitable and generous natured in the world, so it is appreciated when the generosity is reciprocated by bringing a gift when invited to someone's home. However, avoid giving gifts that are obviously expensive or ostentatious, as it will only cause embarrassment and a sense of obligation. Good gift ideas include sweets, chocolate, pastries, decorative hand towels, or flowers. Gifts for the children, such as toys or sweets, will also be welcomed.

As in the many European countries that have colonized the Caribbean, avoid any gifts or flowers that have the colors purple and black, as they are associated with funerals and mourning.

Gift giving is an alternative option to tipping in Cuba, particularly in hotels. Do leave the maid a selection of shampoos and personal care products, as these products are scarce in Cuba and will always be appreciated.

Dressing Etiquette:

Dress etiquette for the Caribbean is definitely relaxed and informal. However, this does not equate to walking around in a bikini and sarong all day. Remember that the Caribbean was colonized by the British, French, and Spanish, which dictated a certain correctness of dress and manners that prevails to this day. Beachwear must only be worn on the beach and around the pool, and make sure that you change out of swimwear as soon as you are off the beach. Otherwise, neat casual attire or sportswear is acceptable. When dining out at a restaurant or at someone's home, make sure that you are dressed in smart-casual attire or evening wear, and are well-groomed.

One's dress and overall appearance is particularly important in the Dominican Republic and Puerto Rico, as it reflects one's success and social status. Although designer brands are favored, this doesn't mean that you need to follow suit. However, do make an effort to be smartly dressed and well groomed if you want to fit in.

Avoid wearing any clothing that is too revealing as the people of the Caribbean are generally modest, particularly as you head more inland. This includes very short shorts and mini-skirts. And definitely do not wear anything that has gratuitous slogans or imagery on it, or resembles military attire.

When visiting religious sites or attending a church service, put on your "Sunday dress," which entails dressing neatly, smartly, modestly, and conservatively. Jeans, t-shirts, shorts, runners/trainers, sleeveless and halter-neck tops are not appropriate and display a lack of respect.

Going topless is acceptable only in some islands of the Caribbean, so work out the lay of the land before you strip off. Otherwise, you could end up offending the locals or, worse, getting pulled up by the authorities. In Barbados and the Cayman Islands, it is actually illegal to go topless. Needless to say that nudity is a no-no in the Caribbean.

Safety Precautions:

Safety precautions differ between regions in the Caribbean, with different degrees of volatility, so always ensure that you look up government updates on the current political situations before traveling.

Always pay close attention to your belongings and personal safety, as the incidence of petty and violent crime in some areas is common. Petty crime such as pick-pocketing and bag snatching occurs, particularly on public transport, intercity buses, major tourist areas, and beaches. Keep valuables such as cameras, mobile phones, and jewelry out of sight. Thefts from hotel and guesthouse accommodation occur.

A high incidence of crime, including armed robbery, kidnapping and murder, is prevalent in some areas of the Caribbean. Violent crime is often gang-related, so it is best to ask the advice of your hotel concierge, or Caribbean host, before you go wandering around on foot, particularly after dark.

Criminals often pose as bogus tour agents or taxi drivers, therefore always use established tour operators and registered taxis.

Avoid placing jewelry, cameras, electronics and other valuable items into your checked luggage. Theft of items from checked baggage at airports has occurred.

Car-related crime is increasing. A common ploy used by thieves is to slash car tires and then assist in repairs, while an accomplice steals from the vehicle. Thieves who pose as hitchhikers are also common.

Driving in some areas can be dangerous, particularly at night, due to inadequate street signs and lighting, and poorly maintained roads and vehicles. If involved in an accident, you are likely to be detained, regardless of who is at fault, and possibly not be allowed to leave the country until the case is resolved.

Avoid using unlicensed private taxis. Use only registered taxis, which can be booked by telephone. Riding mopeds, or three-wheel Coco-Taxis, are not very safe, so my advice is to used registered taxis instead.

Remain vigilant in public areas and avoid public transport or walking or jogging alone, especially after dark. Where possible, you should travel with other people. Use of a reputable tour company or tour organizer may reduce the risks associated with travel in remote areas.

Women, especially if traveling alone, should exercise caution when dealing with strangers or new acquaintances (including hotel employees). Avoid accepting invitations or lifts from strangers, due to the incidences of assault towards foreign women.

Incidents of drink spiking at bars and other entertainment venues have occurred, often resulting in theft and assault. Do not leave your drink unattended.

Using ATMs on the street puts you at high risk of robbery. Changing money at hotels or using ATMs in shopping centers or department stores may reduce this risk. Do not withdraw too much money at any one time, avoid making withdrawals at night and be aware of your surroundings.

It is illegal to smoke and/or use marijuana in Jamaica, and for that matter in the rest of the Caribbean. Although you may get away with a smoke in the privacy of your room, you run the risk of being tricked out of your money when buying it, being lured to remote places and robbed, or having the marijuana laced with a dangerous chemical. Should you have any traces of marijuana, or any other illegal substance, on you or in your luggage, chances are that the sniffer dogs will trace it at the airport, you will get caught, and face prosecution. My strong advice is to steer clear of possessing, buying, selling, or carrying marijuana or any form of illegal drugs while in Jamaica and the Caribbean as you will be committing a serious crime.

Hurricane season is June to November when landslides, mudslides, flooding and disruptions to essential services may occur.

twenty

The United States of America

> "We hold these truths to be self-evident, that all men are created equal, that they are endowed by their Creator with certain unalienable Rights, and that among these are Life, Liberty and the Pursuit of Happiness."
>
> **– THE AMERICAN DECLARATION OF INDEPENDENCE**

Historic Influences:

The Indigenous peoples of North America are the American Indians. Composed of different tribes and ethnic groups, the American Indians lived as hunter gatherers, and passed their stories down by oral traditions. They carried out sophisticated cultivation of various staple crops, such as maize, beans, and squash. After the American Indians, America was occupied by European colonists, who followed the voyages of Christopher Columbus into the "New World" from 1492 onwards. Made up of pilgrims who left England to seek religious freedom in America, the colonies stretched from Maine to Georgia by 1620.

By 1630, a colonial assembly was created to share power with a governor who was appointed by Britain's king. By the 1770s, 13 colonies had developed their own political and legal systems, and were enjoying some measure of prosperity. The 13 colonies were made up of three distinct regions:

- **New England** – Fishing, whaling and shipbuilding were the main industries in this area, which included Massachusetts, New Hampshire, Rhode Island and Connecticut.

- **The Middle Colonies** – This area, which included New York, Delaware, New Jersey and Pennsylvania, mainly produced wheat. Its major cities included New York and Philadelphia.

- **The Southern Colonies** – Mainly producing tobacco, cotton, and indigo, the Southern Colonies were made up of Virginia, Maryland, North Carolina, South Carolina and Georgia, including the ports of Baltimore, Charleston and Jamestown.

While the British felt that the colonies existed for the benefit of the "mother country", the North American colonies grew resentful. Eventually, the British government's threat to American self-government led to war in 1775. Called the American Revolution, financial and military support from France ensured that the patriots won the revolution. At the end of the war, the American Declaration of Independence was signed in 1776, and war hero George Washington became the first president.

After fighting a second war of independence in 1812, there was a general feeling of unity in the country. Known as the "Era of Good Feelings", Republican James Monroe became president.

In the meantime, the importation of Africans as slaves resulted in conflict between the Old and New World societies. Although it was abolished in the North, the heavy world demand for cotton resulted in slavery flourishing in the Southern states, due to its economic advantage. This divided the nation. In 1860, newly elected president Abraham Lincoln called for a stop to slavery, triggering a crisis. The bloody American Civil War ensued (1861–65). With the South eventually defeated, slavery was abolished, equal rights were extended to African Americans, and the American Civil War became the single most iconic event that redefined the history of the United States.

While the South remained poor and African Americans remained socially inferior, the North and West of the United States grew rapidly in the 1900s. The arrival of immigrant workers from Europe led to an outburst of entrepreneurship and an industrial boom. Men such as John D Rockefeller, who dominated the oil industry, and Andrew Carnegie, a captain of industry, amassed incredible personal fortunes. During this era, railroads, automobiles, airplanes, and important inventions, such as the telegraph, the telephone, and light bulb, revolutionized industry as well as everyday life. From the 1890s to the 1920s, reforms such as women's suffrage and the prohibition of alcohol was pushed.

After World War I, Americans became distrustful of foreigners, and immigration slowed right down. Communism paranoia and its influence on American society ensued. Calvin Coolidge, who became president in 1923, encouraged business, which produced a period of great prosperity in the 1920s. However, the Wall Street Crash of 1929 defined the end of the party, marking the onset of the decade-long worldwide Great Depression. The installation of Franklin D Roosevelt as president, along with his elaborate New Deal programs for relief, recovery, and reform, dominated American politics for the decades to come.

The United States entered World War II after the Japanese attacked Pearl Harbor in 1941, and helped the Allied forces in defeating Nazi Germany in Europe, and the Japanese in Asia and in the Pacific. Modern warfare took on a sinister turn with the detonation of the newly-invented atomic bomb on Hiroshima and Nagasaki in 1945, heralding the end of the war.

After the Second World War ended, anti-communist sentiment continued to run at fever pitch. The Cold War between the opposing superpowers, the United States and Russia, began. An arms race, Space Race, and intervention in Europe and eastern Asia, followed. The Cuban Missile Crisis in 1962 was the closest that the country got to nuclear war with the Soviet Union.

After President Kennedy was assassinated in 1963, President Johnson escalated the infamous Vietnam War, where enormous numbers of troops were used to fight communism in Asia. A largely unpopular war with the younger generation, the fiercest opposition came from university students. Back at home, civil rights became hugely important in the 1960s, with great speakers such as Martin Luther King Jr stirring peaceful protest and civil disobedience. As a result, President Johnson pushed through the Civil Rights Act of 1964, a landmark piece of legislation that outlawed major forms of discrimination against blacks and women.

The 1990s brought with it the Information Age, which mushroomed as a result of information technology. This golden era provided yet another boost to the American economy. However, international conflict and economic uncertainty were not far away. The September 11 attacks in 2001, a series of four coordinated suicide attacks upon the United States committed by 19 militants associated with the Islamic extremist group al-Qaeda, shocked the nation to its roots. This was followed by the "War on Terror," a phrase coined by President George W Bush that applied to the campaign waged against al-Qaeda and other militant organizations. In 2007, the speculative bubble in real estate and equities burst, highlighting Wall Street's risky lending practices and exposing weaknesses in the American political institutions.

The on-going war in the Middle East, combined with the global financial crisis, has undoubtedly placed heavy burdens on the US economy. However, American optimism, ambition, determination and the right to the pursuit of happiness, as much a part of the American collective DNA as breathing, can hopefully ensure the country's resurrection.

Greeting & Conversation Etiquette:

Americans are open, gregarious, and hospitable . Their style is generally relaxed, informal, and they are not ones to stand on ceremony. If you come from an Anglo-Saxon background, you may find their manner and conversation style refreshing. However, visitors from more formal or patriarchal backgrounds may find this level of openness confronting.

Reflecting their casual style, Americans prefer to be called by their first names straight away. However, in the business or official arena, it is always best to use their title (e.g., Mr, Mrs, Ms., Dr, Professor) followed by their last name, until you've been given permission to do otherwise. *Sir* or *Madam* may also be used in higher end restaurants/hotels, or when addressing people to whom greater respect should be shown, such as a politician, elderly person, or boss. The term *ma'am* is a more colloquial version of *madam* when an elderly lady is being addressed.

In more formal or official settings, American men and women greet each other with a brief but firm handshake, accompanied with direct eye contact and a smile. In social events, however, handshakes are dispensed with, and are replaced with a smile, direct eye contact, and a greeting such as "hello," or "hi, how are you?" Unlike the Russians or Germans, who will take "how are you" as a literal enquiry into their health, the Americans see this as a mere pleasantry. The simplest way to respond to this is "fine, thank you" or even "great".

Unlike the French, who find group waves socially unacceptable, waving when saying "hello" or "goodbye" to people in a social setting is acceptable in the United States. It's done by moving the entire hand from left to right, with the palm facing outward.

People from the Mediterranean, take note. Americans keep a personal space distance of about two feet (roughly arm's length), so keep your distance when conversing. However, the distance will shorten the more comfortable they are with you, and the better acquainted you become with your American friend.

With regards to touching, hugging, and kissing, Americans only do this with family members and close friends in social occasions, as they are considered intimate gestures. You definitely know you've made a friend when an American gives you a backslap or bear hug. When you've gotten to know your American friends well, a kiss is given on one cheek. Only lovers kiss on the mouth.

Being polite is a "must" in the United States. As in Great Britain, saying "please" and "thank you" are very important to the Americans, as are "Pardon me" or "excuse me," which can be used when they do not understand something or when they bump into someone. Failure to say these words at the appropriate times, or often enough, can lead to someone being perceived as rude.

Americans are great at small talk and social chit chat. They will more than likely get uncomfortable if someone delves too deeply into a particular topic in a casual encounter. A good rule of thumb is to keep it brief, pleasant, and light.

Having that, Americans can sometimes delve into extremely private matters, or ask extremely personal questions, which can end up making you slightly uncomfortable if you come from a more formal culture. Should this happen, it's perfectly OK to say "If you don't mind, I'd rather not discuss it" or "It's a little personal." The Americans' openness and transparency gives them an appreciation for direct honesty, so they will not take offense.

Americans may have an open demeanor and be quick with the smiles. However, they say what they mean and mean what they say. "No" always means no. Not "maybe," or "perhaps," or "ask me again later." It means "No, and do not ask again." Many a Mediterranean or Eastern European man can attest to being slapped or told off after not taking "no" for an answer.

When saying goodbye, Americans like to say "see you later" or "let's catch up." This is meant to be a pleasantry so do not take it literally. Unless a date and time is specified, the invitation isn't a firm one. Should you want to follow up with your American friend, it's best that you instigate the next invitation or get-together.

Conversation Taboos:

- Americans are, on the whole, more conservative than the British and Australians. Definite conversation taboos include sex, religion, abortion, politics, and racism.

- Americans are also very patriotic, and are proud of their country and culture. To criticize their government, country, culture, or someone's patriotism constitutes a major *faux pas*. You will know if you have crossed that line in no uncertain terms.

Appropriate Social Behavior:

"I love America more than any other country in this world; and, exactly for this reason, I insist on the right to criticize her perpetually."

– JAMES BALDWIN, AMERICAN NOVELIST, ESSAYIST, PLAYWRIGHT, POET, AND SOCIAL CRITIC.

Americans smile. A lot. All the time. Even at strangers. The French, British, Germans, and Russians may find this strange, even at times annoying. However, this is a sign from the Americans that all is well, and they are happy with themselves and the world at that moment in time. Do return the smile. You'll find that it will lift your day and put you in a different space. If there's ever a habit that the world can afford to pick up from the Americans, it's this one.

Americans have no taboos around showing the soles of their feet or shoes. As a result, men and women usually sit with legs crossed at the ankles or knees, or even one ankle crossed on the knee for some men.

Unlike Europe, where every man and his dog will defend their right to smoke, smoking is very unpopular in the United States. Forget about lighting up inside someone's home, unless you're outside, and even then, not without the host's permission. Although many restaurants may have separate non-smoking sections, any whiff of smoke inside the premises will draw disapproving glares and hostile comments from the other patrons. In a nutshell, ask first before lighting up.

Americans are as fastidious about their personal hygiene as they are polite, and if there are certain things that they won't tolerate, it's body odor, unwashed hair, and bad breath (hence their seeming obsession with chewing gum). Most Americans will also have a strong reaction to armpit or leg hair on a woman. Whether you shave your body hair or not is entirely your choice. However, if you know that you'll be doing intense physical exercise, or you are going to sweat profusely, make sure that you shower and throw on some fresh clothes before meeting up with your American friends. And never, ever forget your deodorant.

Unlike the Middle East, gestures like the thumbs up, "OK sign," and "peace" or "victory" signs are totally acceptable. The "shaka" gesture – folding all the fingers except the thumb and pinky, with the back of the hand facing the person being greeted – means "hang loose" or "hello," and is particularly common with surfers and Hawaiians.

Dining Etiquette:

Dinner or lunch at an American home is often a relaxed and informal affair. The food may be served buffet style if the numbers are larger, or platters passed from person to person if the numbers are smaller. With their plethora of sauces, marinades, salads, and grills, Americans have elevated their barbecues, or "cookouts", into an art form.

Americans value punctuality, and view lateness as a sign of rudeness. It's acceptable to arrive up to 15 minutes after the invited time. However, a phone call with an apology is warranted if you will be delayed for more than that. Arriving too early is considered just as rude, as you'll be interrupting your host's preparations.

While Europeans typically eat Continental style, which is the fork on the left hand and the knife on the right, Americans will eat with the hand that they write with, or their dominant hand. It is common for them to cut up their food into bite sized pieces with the fork on the left and knife on the right. Then, they will switch the fork back to the dominant hand, scoop or spear the food with the fork tines facing up, and bring the food up to their mouths. Having said that, eating Continental style is perfectly acceptable.

The napkin (or serviette) is placed on your lap shortly after you are seated, and is kept on your lap all throughout the meal. Do not tuck your napkin under your chin.

Unlike the formal European dining culture, it is perfectly acceptable in the United States to have your hands resting on your lap when you aren't eating. This is more for comfort than anything else.

Women and elderly people are served at the table before anyone else. It's also polite to offer people around you food and drink before you help yourself. Eating or drinking doesn't usually begin until the host is seated and begins. Americans love to see you enjoying their food, so feel free to go for second helpings.

Eating a pizza is done with a knife and fork at first, at least while the dish is still hot. Once part of the pizza is eaten, and the crust has cooled down considerably, then it's acceptable to pick the slice up with your hands. Likewise, sandwiches and hamburgers are eaten with the hands. Don't be too fussed if bits of meat and vegetables slip out either, as that's what the plates and napkins are for.

When you are done eating, simply leave a small amount of food on your plate and leave your fork and knife to the side of your plate.

When eating out at a restaurant, it is common to ask the waiter to pack any left-over food in a box or bag to take away with you. This makes perfect sense as the American food portions are larger than normal.

When eating out in the United States, the one that invites is the one that pays. Tipping is also a must, as waiters and waitresses are not paid a high base salary, and depend on their tips to supplement their income. Tips are generally 20% of the bill.

Valets in hotels and car parks are also given tips of, say, US$5 after they have collected your car. Housekeepers in hotels are normally tipped about US$20, which is given to them at the end of the guest's stay.

Gift Giving Etiquette:

Although Americans do not have the tradition of gift giving that, say, the Japanese have, it is customary to bring your host something when you have been invited to their home for lunch or dinner. A lovely box of chocolates, fruit basket, a good bottle of wine, a bunch of flowers, or a potted plant are all good ideas. Gifts from your country, like a coffee table book, good quality craft, or specialty food will always be appreciated. Make sure that they are well presented and attractively wrapped.

Regarding certain colors and flowers, they do not have the cultural taboo in the United States that they do in some countries.

Dressing Etiquette:

As personal hygiene is of paramount importance to the Americans, so is personal grooming. They do not appreciate untidiness, or clothes that look tattered, unpressed, or old.

American women, in general, have a neat, wholesome, and natural style. Day wear can range from jeans and a lovely top when walking around, to simple dresses and/or coordinated pieces when invited to someone's home for a meal or eating out. It's never seen as appropriate to overdress during the day, or wear flashy, over-the-top jewelry.

An evening invitation, depending on the city you are in and where you will be going, will call for something a little dressier. Whether you're in a dress or pants, always go for an uncluttered, understated look when dressing in the United States. Overly revealing clothes, such as low-cut blouses, extremely short skirts, and overly tight skirts, pants, or dresses, never reflect well on the wearer.

Safety Precautions:

The United States is a relatively safe place to travel to, so there is no need to continually look over your shoulder, despite the easy availability of handguns.

However, like all countries in the world, there are certain areas that are more disadvantaged than others, which then attracts higher levels of crime. "Drive-by" shootings only occur in the neighborhoods where gang conflicts are common. If you have any doubts as to whether it's safe for you to walk around or not, simply ask your host or concierge at your hotel. It is never a good idea for a woman to walk around on her own at night anyway.

Private property is taken very seriously in the United States. Never trespass or camp in private property. Stay on public beaches, marked trails, and State or National Parks, and consult your guidebook for designated wilderness areas, where camping is permitted. You'd be getting off lightly if you were fined or even arrested – remember those relaxed gun laws.

If you're a woman, avoid drinking in bars that have a mostly male crowd, even if you are with another female friend. You could be perceived as "looking for company" and may attract some harassment.

twenty-one

Travel Quotations

You've planned your journey, taken care of all the essentials and practicalities like ticketing and packing, you've researched the culture that you will be visiting, and you have planned your itinerary extensively. Now what you have to do is savor the journey!

I have listed a total of 118 travel quotes below for you to enjoy. May I suggest that you pick a travel quote for the day and keep the message in your heart as you make the most of your travels.

And last but not least, safe travels!

"The world is a book, and those who do not travel read only a page."

– ST. AUGUSTINE.

"We wander for distraction, but we travel for fulfillment."

– HILAIRE BELLOC.

"Half the fun of travel is the aesthetic of lostness."

– RAY BRADBURY

"I soon realized that no journey carries one far unless, as it extends into the world around us, it goes an equal distance into the world within."

– LILLIAN SMITH.

"Blessed are the curious for they shall have adventures."

– LOVELLE DRACHMAN.

"As you grow older, you'll find that the only things you regret are the things you didn't do."

– ZACHARY SCOTT.

"Do not be too squeamish about your actions. All life is an experience."

– RALPH WALDO EMERSON.

"The first step in the journey is to lose your way."

– GALWAY KINNELL.

"Life is either a daring adventure or nothing."

– HELEN KELLER.

"Wandering re-establishes the original harmony which once existed between man and the universe."

– ANATOLE FRANCE.

"Every one of us has in him a continent of undiscovered character."

– CHARLES L WALLIS.

"To travel hopefully is a better thing than to arrive."

– ROBERT LOUIS STEVENSON.

"No one realizes how beautiful it is to travel until he comes home and rests his head on his old, familiar pillow."

– LIN YUTANG.

Any place that we love becomes our world.

– OSCAR WILDE.

"The whole object of travel is not to set foot on foreign land; it is at last to set foot on one's own country as a foreign land."

– G.K. CHESTERTON.

"Every step of the journey is the journey."

– ZEN SAYING.

"Look closely. The beautiful may be small."

– EMMANUEL KANT.

"As long as habit and routine dictate the pattern of living, new dimensions of the soul will not emerge."

— HENRY VAN DYKE.

"The aim of life is to live, and to live means to be aware, joyously, drunkenly, divinely aware."

— HENRY MILLER.

"Some experiences simply do not translate. You have to go to know."

— KOBI YAMADA.

"Seek and you will find. Don't be willing to accept an ordinary life."

— SALLE MERRILL REDFIELD.

"One doesn't discover new lands without consenting to lose sight of the shore for a very long time."

— ANDRE GIDE.

"Discoveries are often made by not following instructions, by going off the main road, by trying the untried."

— FRANK TYGER.

"The purpose of education is to replace an empty mind with an open one."

— MALCOLM FORBES.

"People travel to wonder at the height of mountains, at the huge waves of the sea, at the long course of rivers, and they pass by themselves – without wondering."

– ST. AUGUSTINE.

"Wake up and live."

– BOB MARLEY

"Life, we learn too late, is in the living, the tissue of every day and hour."

– STEPHEN B. LEACOOKE.

"A man who views the world at 50 the same as he did at 20 has wasted 30 years of his life."

– MUHAMMAD ALI.

"Imagination is a poor substitute for experience."

– HAVELOCK ELLIS.

"It is only in adventure that some people succeed in knowing themselves – in finding themselves."

– ANDRE GIDE.

"An original life is unexplored territory. You don't get there taking a taxi – you get there by carrying a canoe."

– ALAN ALDA.

"A frontier is never a place; it is a time, an attitude, and a way of life."

– HAL BORLAND.

"My favorite thing is to go where I've never been."

– DIANE ARBUS.

"Laughter has no foreign accent."

– PAUL LOWNEY.

"The fool wonders, the wise man wanders."

– SUSAN REA.

"Life is not a problem to be solved, but a mystery to be lived."

– THOMAS MERTON.

"Those who wander are not necessarily lost."

– KOBI YAMADA.

"Without experience, there is little wisdom."

– APOCRYPHA.

"Certainly, travel is more than the seeing of sights; it is a change that goes on, deep and permanent, in the ideas of living."

– MIRIAM BEARD.

"This is what travel is all about. We strain to renew our capacity for wonder, to shock ourselves into astonishment once again."

– SHANA ALEXANDER.

"To awaken in a strange town is one of the most pleasant sensations in the world."

– FREYA STARK.

"The true fruit of travel is perhaps the feeling of being nearly everywhere at home."

– FREYA STARK.

"The place you have left forever is always there for you to see whenever you shut your eyes."

– HAMILTON HENNING.

"Trips don't end when we return home – in a sense it's when they usually begin."

– AGNES E BENEDICT.

"Be as the stars in the sky, ask neither when nor why."

– VICTORIA UGARTE.

"I love to explore and taste and imagine."

– OLIVER SACKS.

"Every now and then go away and have a little relaxation. To remain constantly at work will diminish your judgment. Go some distance away, because work will be in perspective and a lack of harmony is more readily seen."

– LEONARDO DA VINCI.

"Improve your spare moments and they will become the brightest gems in your life."

– RALPH WALDO EMERSON.

"When the days are too short, chances are you are living at your best."

– EARL NIGHTINGALE.

"If the Earth were only a few feet in diameter, floating a few feet above a field somewhere, people would come from everywhere to marvel at it, declare it sacred and protect it."

– JOE MILLER.

"I have just dropped into the very place I have been seeking, but in everything it exceeds all my dreams."

– ISABELLA BIRD.

"He who would travel happily must travel light."

– ANTOINE DE SAINT-EXUPERY.

"We are all travelers in the wilderness of this world, and the best that we find in our travels is an honest friend."

– ROBERT LOUIS STEVENSON.

"Fear makes strangers out of people who should be friends."

– SHIRLEY MACLAINE.

"Once in a while it really hits people that they don't have to experience the world in the way they have been told to."

– ALAN KEIGHTLEY.

"Everything I learn makes me see how much more there is to know and how little time there is in a lifetime to learn it all."

– TOM BROWN JR.

"Twenty years from now, you will be more disappointed by the things you didn't do than by the ones you did do. So throw off the bowlines, sail away from the safe harbor. Catch the trade winds in your sails. Explore. Dream. Discover."

– MARK TWAIN.

"You have brains in your head and feet in your shoes. You can steer yourself any direction you choose. You're on your own and you know what you know. And you are the one who'll decide where to go."

– DR SUESS.

"The reason for any journey is this: in a journey, discoveries are made."

– KOBI YAMADA.

"It doesn't matter what road you take, hill you climb, or path you're on, you will always end up in the same place, learning."

"One small step up the mountain often widens your horizon in all directions."

– EH GRIGGS.

"The road of life can only reveal itself as it is travelled; each turn in the road reveals a surprise. Man's future is hidden."

– MARTIN MUELLER.

"If the future road looks ominous or unpromising, and the roads back uninviting, then we need to gather our resolve and, carrying only the necessary baggage, step off that road into another direction."

– MAYA ANGELOU.

"It's not trespassing if the boundaries you cross are your own."

– ALLYSON MOORE.

"No matter how far a person can go, the horizon is still way beyond you."

– ZORA NEALE HURSTON.

"We leave behind a bit of ourselves wherever we've been."

– EDMOND HARACOURT.

"He who returns from a journey is not the same as he who left."

– CHINESE PROVERB.

"I travel not to go anywhere, but to go. I travel for travel's sake. The great affair is to move."

– ROBERT LOUIS STEVENSON.

"The real voyage of discovery consists not in seeking new landscapes but in having new eyes."

– MARCEL PROUST.

"The longest journey a man must take is the 18 inches from his head to his heart."

– UNKNOWN.

"A good traveler has no fixed plans, and is not intent on arriving."

– LAO TZU

"A man travels the world in search of what he needs and returns home to find it."

– GEORGE MOORE.

"Experience, travel – these are an education in themselves."

– EURIPIDES.

"Your lost friends are not dead, but gone before, advanced a stage or two upon that road which you must travel in the steps they trod."

– ARISTOPHANES.

"Only he that has traveled the road knows where the holes are deep."

– CHINESE PROVERB.

"Two roads diverged in the wood, and I – I took the one less traveled by, and that has made all the difference."

– ROBERT FROST.

"Perhaps travel cannot prevent bigotry, but by demonstrating that all peoples cry, laugh, eat, worry, and die, it can introduce the idea that if we try and understand each other, we may even become friends."

– MAYA ANGELOU.

"All journeys have secret destinations of which the traveler is unaware."

– MARTIN BUBER.

"I see my path, but I don't know where it leads. Not knowing where I'm going is what inspires me to travel it."

— ROSALIA DE CASTRO.

"I travel a lot; I hate my life disrupted by routine."

— CASKIE STINNETT.

"It is better to travel than to arrive."

— UNKNOWN.

"The great difference between voyages rests not with the ships, but with the people you meet on them."

— AMELIA E BARR.

Living on Earth may be expensive, but it includes an annual free trip around the sun.

— UNKNOWN.

Never go on trips with anyone you do not love.

— ERNEST HEMINGWAY.

"We may run, walk, stumble, drive, or fly, but let us never lose sight of the reason for the journey, or miss a chance to see a rainbow on the way."

— UNKNOWN.

"Travel teaches toleration."

— BENJAMIN DISRAELI.

"My travels led me to where I am today. Sometimes these steps have felt painful, difficult, but led me to greater happiness and opportunities."

– DIANA ROSS.

"Travel, in the younger sort, is a part of education; in the elder, a part of experience."

– FRANCIS BACON SR.

"Like all great travelers, I have seen more than I remember, and remember more than I have seen."

– BENJAMIN DISRAELI.

"The man who goes alone can start today; but he who travels with another must wait till that other is ready."

– HENRY DAVID THOREAU.

"Travel only with thy equals or thy betters; if there are none, travel alone."

– THE DHAMMAPADA.

"When you travel, remember that a foreign country is not designed to make you comfortable. It is designed to make its own people comfortable."

– CLIFTON FADIMAN.

"Travel and change of place imparts new vigor to the mind."

– SENECA.

"The rewards of the journey far outweigh the risk of leaving the harbor."

– UNKNOWN.

"I may not have gone where I intended to go, but I think I have ended up where I intended to be."

– DOUGLAS ADAMS.

"When you get there, there isn't any there there."

– GERTRUDE STEIN.

"It is no coincidence that in no known language does the phrase, "As pretty as an airport" appear."

– DOUGLAS ADAMS.

"Tourists don't know where they've been, travelers don't know where they're going."

– PAUL THEROUX.

"One always begins to forgive a place as soon as it's left behind."

– CHARLES DICKENS.

"Too often travel, instead of broadening the mind, merely lengthens the conversation."

– ELIZABETH DREW.

"Two great talkers will not travel far together."

– SPANISH PROVERB.

"I love to travel but hate to arrive."

– ALBERT EINSTEIN.

"A journey of a thousand miles begins with a single step."

– CONFUCIUS.

"Don't tell me how educated you are, tell me how much you have traveled."

– MOHAMMED.

"Own only what you can carry with you; let your memory be your travel bag."

– ALEXANDER SOLZHENITSYN.

"It is solved by walking."

– ALGERIAN PROVERB.

"A journey is like marriage. The certain way to be wrong is to think you control it."

– JOHN STEINBECK.

"A wise traveler never despises his own country."

– CARLO GOLDONI.

"I should like to spend the whole of my life in traveling abroad, if I could anywhere borrow another life to spend afterwards at home."

– WILLIAM HAZLITT.

"A traveler to distant places should make no enemies."

"Everywhere is nowhere. When a person spends all his time in foreign travel, he ends by having many acquaintances, but no friends."

— SENECA.

"Journeys, like artists, are born and not made. A thousand differing circumstances contribute to them, few of them willed or determined by the will — whatever we may think."

— LAWRENCE DURRELL.

"Travel makes a wise man better, and a fool worse."

— THOMAS FULLER.

"A holiday is over when you begin to yearn for your work."

— MORRIS FISHBEIN.

"Every perfect traveler always creates the country where he travels."

— NIKOS KAZANTZAKIS.

"We live in a wonderful world that is full of beauty, charm and adventure. There is no end to the adventures we can have if we only seek them with our eyes open."

— JAWAHARAL NEHRU

"May you always find new roads to travel, new horizons to explore, new dreams to call your own."

— UNKNOWN.

THANK YOU!

Thank you for buying and reading this book, and trusting me to offer you something of value. I sincerely hope that you use this information to make your travels throughout the world as enriching as possible, and that you too will grow to love the myriad of cultures and experiences it has to offer.

I'd be thrilled to hear from you, and about all your travel adventures. You may even want to send me your travel story to publish on my website. I'd be delighted! All you need to do is visit my website, www.ExploreMyWorldTravel.com and click on the 'Contact' button. Easy. And from there, our friendship will start.

I hope that you'll consider subscribing to my blog or sending me a comment through Amazon. I'd consider it a great honor. That would let me know that you enjoyed this book and that it made some impact on your life.

If your sense of adventure is still calling, then you may also be interested in my other books, filled with more valuable travel tips, resources and anecdotes:

The Travel Bible For Women

Discover Sydney's Bondi Beach: A Guide For Fashionistas & Foodies

A Foodie & Fashionista's Guide To London

ACKNOWLEDGMENTS

I seem to have spent my whole life researching this book, with various family members and friends providing rich fodder for its content.

I am thankful for my paternal grandparents, Marcelino Ugarte and Ana Aboitiz Ugarte, and maternal grandparents, Ernesto Ghezzi and Remedios Salado Ghezzi, for the richness of their collective Basque/ Castilian/ Northern Italian heritage, and for giving in to their spirit of adventure and migrating to the Philippines in the 1890's. This afforded my parents, and all of us children, all the blessings that came with European roots coupled with a Southeast Asian upbringing.

I am forever grateful to my parents, Sebastian Ugarte and Julia Ghezzi Ugarte, for inspiring me to value and appreciate the people and culture of other lands and planting the seeds of the travel bug in me. Our home was always filled with colorful dignitaries and foreign guests, exposing my brothers and I to different cultures, accents and customs. Their children became my playmates, and after returning to their own countries, turned into my penpals (yes, we did write letters in those days). As my parents traveled the globe extensively, they always brought me back a souvenir of a doll in the national costume of their host country. I have the dolls to this day.

I am also grateful for my father's foresight in relocating us as a family from the Philippines to Australia, and my mother for having the courage to execute the move on her own in 1976, a mere two years after my father's death. Australia, a country where all nationalities and cultures are embraced and welcomed, has been good to us as a family. Extensive immigration from countries and cultures from around the world through the decades has extended the cultural diversity of this nation, making it one of the most diverse populations in the world today. I consider myself fortunate to be living here, and to have raised my son in a country that embraces diversity.

My childhood years seemed to have been spent, with my younger brother Eduardo, waiting for my older brothers to come home from their studies or travels abroad: Xavier from his trips to the United States and Europe, and Juan Miguel from Sydney, Australia. This instilled in me an even greater yearning to spread my wings. Years later, I am grateful to my sister-in-laws, Rebeca Salvatierra Ugarte and Clare Hannigan Ugarte, for giving me insights into their own cultures, Chilean and Australian respectively, drawing my brothers and I into their cultural heritage and network of friends.

Aside from the Philippines, the Ugarte-Ghezzi clan are spread all over the world, which gave me the opportunity in my youth to spend time in, and forge strong emotional ties with, Italy, Spain, and the United States. While completing my design degree in Florida (United States) in 1984, my Colombian room mate, Liliana Tovar, as well as a plethora of friends from South and Central America, gave me a wonderful understanding of the *Latino* customs and outlook on life. And after giving birth to my son, Justin, during that year, my Jamaican friend Ruth Bajnauth generously offered for us to stay in their home until I completed my studies. Their kindness, generosity, and passion for music and living has forever etched the Jamaican ethos and way of life into my, and my son's, heart.

I consider myself fortunate to have spent time working in the Myer Fashion Office and at Rapee Pty. Ltd. My jobs with both companies had me traveling the world extensively, giving me the opportunity to interact and conduct business with men and women from the four corners of the world and learning from my cultural mistakes in a protected environment.

Thanks goes to those wonderful people whose brains I have picked in the course of writing this book. Ilana Barda and Zevic Mishor for their invaluable input on Israel, Mariam Issa for her knowledge on the Middle East and its Muslim customs, Barbara Schaffer on South Africa, Ruby Madan on India, and Kathrin Luty on Germany.

To my younger brother and the best editor I know, Dr Eduardo F. Ugarte. Thank you for taming my penchant for hyperbole with efficiency coupled with great sensitivity.

I have been embraced by the Greek culture through Justin's wife, and my daughter-in-law, Maryanne Apostolou Ugarte. The copious Greek Easters and Christmas celebrations that we have spent in her parents, Con and Maria Apostolou's, home have not only added inches to our waistline but have upped the ante on generosity and hospitality.

To my loyal gang of five - my amazing son Justin and his lovely wife Maryanne, my vibrant step-daughter Natasha and her gorgeous son Jakob, and thoughtful step-son Nick - for your love, support, nurturing and constant source of entertainment. How blessed am I to have all of you in my life.

Finally, my deepest gratitude goes to my wonderful husband, best friend, biggest fan and partner-in-crime, Peter Borsky. Born and bred in Prague, in the Czech Republic, as well as opening up my world to the culture and customs of Eastern Europe, he has been my tireless travel buddy and patron of the arts (my arts!), exploring the world with me and encouraging me to follow my dreams. *De^kuji!*

19719097R00160

Made in the USA
Lexington, KY
06 January 2013